SMART GUIDE

CREATIVE
HOMEOWNER®

home landscaping

CREATIVE HOMEOWNER®, Upper Saddle River, New Jersey

SMART GUIDE: HOME LANDSCAPING

TECHNICAL EDITOR	Miranda Smith
SENIOR GRAPHIC DESIGN COORDINATOR	Glee Barre
JUNIOR EDITOR	Jennifer Calvert
PHOTO COORDINATOR	Robyn Poplasky
INDEXER	Schroeder Indexing Services
DIGITAL IMAGING SPECIALIST	Frank Dyer
FRONT COVER PHOTOGRAPHY	Gill Hanley/Garden Picture Library
SMART GUIDE® SERIES COVER DESIGN	Clarke Barre

CREATIVE HOMEOWNER

VICE PRESIDENT AND PUBLISHER	Timothy O. Bakke
ART DIRECTOR	David Geer
MANAGING EDITOR	Fran J. Donegan

Current Printing (last digit)
10 9 8 7 6 5 4 3

Manufactured in the United States of America

Smart Guide: Home Landscaping, First Edition
Library of Congress Control Number: 2008921443
ISBN-10: 1-58011-421-0
ISBN-13: 978-1-58011-421-9

CREATIVE HOMEOWNER®
A Division of Federal Marketing Corp.
24 Park Way
Upper Saddle River, NJ 07458
www.creativehomeowner.com

Metric Conversion

Length

1 inch	25.4 mm
1 foot	0.3048 m
1 yard	0.9144 m
1 mile	1.61 km

Area

1 square inch	645 mm²
1 square foot	0.0929 m²
1 square yard	0.8361 m²
1 acre	4046.86 m²
1 square mile	2.59 km²

Volume

1 cubic inch	16.3870 cm³
1 cubic foot	0.03 m³
1 cubic yard	0.77 m³

Common Lumber Equivalents

Sizes: Metric cross sections are so close to their U.S. sizes, as noted below, that for most purposes they may be considered equivalents.

Dimensional lumber	1 x 2	19 x 38 mm
	1 x 4	19 x 89 mm
	2 x 2	38 x 38 mm
	2 x 4	38 x 89 mm
	2 x 6	38 x 140 mm
	2 x 8	38 x 184 mm
	2 x 10	38 x 235 mm
	2 x 12	38 x 286 mm
Sheet sizes	4 x 8 ft.	1200 x 2400 mm
	4 x 10 ft.	1200 x 3000 mm
Sheet thicknesses	¼ in.	6 mm
	⅜ in.	9 mm
	½ in.	12 mm
	¾ in.	19 mm
Stud/joist spacing	16 in. o.c.	400 mm o.c.
	24 in. o.c.	600 mm o.c.

Capacity

1 fluid ounce	29.57 mL
1 pint	473.18 mL
1 quart	1.14 L
1 gallon	3.79 L

Weight

1 ounce	28.35g
1 pound	0.45kg

Temperature

Celsius = Fahrenheit – 32 x $\frac{5}{9}$
Fahrenheit = Celsius x 1.8 + 32

contents

safety first

All projects and procedures in this book have been reviewed for safety; still it is not possible to overstate the importance of working carefully. What follows are reminders for plant care and project safety. Always use common sense.

■ *Always* use caution, care, and good judgment when following the procedures in this book.

■ *Always* determine locations of underground utility lines before you dig, and then avoid them by a safe distance. Buried lines may be for gas, electricity, communications, or water. Contact local utility companies who will help you map their lines.

■ *Always* read and heed tool manufacturer instructions.

■ *Always* ensure that the electrical setup is safe; be sure that no circuit is overloaded and that all power tools and electrical outlets are properly grounded and protected by a ground-fault circuit interrupter (GCFI). Do not use power tools in wet locations.

■ *Always* wear eye protection when using chemicals, sawing wood, pruning trees and shrubs, using power tools, and striking metal onto metal or concrete.

■ *Always* consider nontoxic and least toxic methods of addressing unwanted plants, plant pests, and plant diseases before resorting to toxic methods. Follow package application and safety instructions carefully.

■ *Always* read labels on chemicals, solvents, and other products; provide ventilation; heed warnings.

■ *Always* wear a hard hat when working in situations with potential for injury from falling tree limbs.

■ *Always* wear appropriate gloves in situations in which your hands could be injured by rough surfaces, sharp edges, thorns, or poisonous plants.

■ *Always* protect yourself against ticks, which can carry Lyme disease. Wear light-colored, long-sleeved shirts and pants. Inspect yourself for ticks after every session in the garden.

■ *Always* wear a disposable face mask or a special filtering respirator when creating sawdust or working with toxic gardening substances.

■ *Always* keep your hands and other body parts away from the business end of blades, cutters, and bits.

■ *Always* obtain approval from local building officials before undertaking construction of permanent structures.

■ *Never* employ herbicides, pesticides, or toxic chemicals unless you have determined with certainty that they were developed for the specific problem you hope to remedy.

■ *Never* allow bystanders to approach work areas where they might by injured by workers or work-site hazards. Be sure work areas are well marked.

■ *Never* work with power tools when you are tired, or under the influence of alcohol or drugs.

■ *Never* carry sharp or pointed tools, such as knives or saws, in your pocket.

Exterior Design

To many of us, the property surrounding our houses is just as important as the rooms in the building. *Smart Guide: Home Landscaping* can help make the most of your exterior living areas by providing a plan to get you started on creating a new landscape or reviving an existing one. This concise guide lays out the steps for developing a landscape design that takes into account the uniqueness of your property as well as the local microclimate. But the book isn't only about planning. If you lack suitable areas for planting or recreation, the guide explains how to improve the soil, terrace your yard, and provide proper drainage and irrigation. It also shows the importance of adding structure to your yard. Garden and retaining walls, fences, gates, and trellises are all important vertical design elements that can be as attractive as they are functional. Of course, landscapes are about plants and *Smart Guide: Home Landscaping* provides information on selecting, planting, and maintaining the backbone of any landscape—the trees and shrubs. The chapter on lawns contains practical tips on growing and caring for lawns of all types. The section on flowers discusses garden and border design, and choosing the best plants for your yard.

creating a plan

The Master Plan

Creating a master landscaping plan will serve as a basic road map for your project. This plan is basically an overhead map of your property that shows its features, including your intended plantings. Whether you wish to landscape your property all at once or plant one section at a time as budget and schedule allow, it is a good idea to create a detailed master plan.

Examine Your Property

Before you draw the plan, make a site analysis of your property. This is simply an inventory of all features that relate to the present landscape. Record this information on a base map, drawn to scale. (See page 9.) The map should show your property boundaries as well as your house and any other structures. Even if you opt to employ a professional designer for the landscape plan, you'd be wise to record information yourself on the site analysis.

A site analysis is an inventory of the features on a property, including any structures, major trees and specimen plants, utility easements, equipment such as air-conditioner units, and the topography of the lot—significant slopes, dips, and hills. A really thorough analysis will also record any aesthetic factors, including attractive or unsightly views, and information on conditions that affect plant growth.

Most homeowners can record the necessary information in a couple of hours. However, if you are new to the property and it is already planted, you may want to record changes throughout a whole year in order to get a true sense of your property.

Kinds of Information to Gather.

"Useful Information" on page 10 lists important information to gather. Although the list is long and comprehensive, don't feel overwhelmed. A site analysis will greatly help you in making informed design decisions. Simply use the text as a

Turn a utilitarian side entrance into a pleasant landscape feature, as the homeowners did with this pretty dooryard garden. Petunias, lobelia, nasturtium, and snapdragons soften the pavement and steps, and make the entrance inviting.

Drawing a master plan of your property will help generate ideas for your landscape plan. For example, a rectangular lot is a good place for a formal garden as shown here.

The most direct route from the driveway to the front door is across the lawn. Here the homeowner laid a stepping-stone path across the route, which saves the grass from wear and tear and keeps shoes dry.

guide, and disregard items that do not apply. However, bear in mind that an accurate site analysis can prevent expensive design errors.

Place Lot Boundaries

If you're starting with an official drawing of your lot, it will show property boundaries accurately. You can next measure other useful distances that aren't recorded on the plat, or property survey, and write them down. For example, you will want to know the length of the front walk, the size of an existing patio, the distance from the patio to the back of the lot, and so on. If the surveyors' pipes or markers are no longer in place, be sure that you find and indicate the exact locations of property corners and edges. (You may need the help of a surveyor to do this.) An error of even a few inches beyond your property line can lead to a dispute with the affected neighbor, especially if you build a fence or plant a hedge. If you don't have an existing plat to work from, measure the property carefully, and draw the boundaries to scale on graph paper. With your boundaries correctly drawn, you'll have a bird's-eye view of your property.

The House

On the plat, draw the perimeter, or footprint, of the ground floor of your house. Note doors leading outside, windows, chimneys, stoops, overhangs, eaves, the garage, and other outbuildings. Indicate dimensions of each feature as close to scale as possible. Also record the height from the ground to the first-floor windowsills. A common mistake is to put plants that will grow too big under windows.

Other Structures

Draw other existing structures such as gazebos, fences, walls, hedges, swing sets, and sandboxes, as well as patios, terraces, decks, ponds, and pools. Lastly, draw in the driveway, walkways, and garden paths, noting the types of paving material.

You can create a base map from a copy of your plat prepared by surveyors, which most homeowners receive when they purchase their house. A plat typically shows several individual properties and may or may not show structures, including houses. If you don't have a plat, request one from your tax assessor's office; copies are usually available at no cost or for a nominal fee.

In addition to showing locations of property lines, a footprint of the house, and any other significant structures, the plat should show easements and the location of overhead and underground utility lines owned by the county or city. It should also have a legend indicating its drawing scale, which is typically 1:20, meaning that every inch on the paper is equivalent to 20 feet on your property. If the scale isn't shown, you can calculate it by measuring a distance on the plat in inches, and then correlating that with the same actual distance on your property.

Make Several Enlarged Copies.

Property surveys and plats are usually a standard size, which is tiny considering all the information you want to record. Take your plat or

property survey to a copy shop or blueprint company to get an enlargement. While you're there, you might as well have them make four or five copies, one for your site analysis, one for drawing your design, and extras for updates and changes over the years. If you can, have the blueprint company enlarge the original scale to at least 1:12. This will give you more room to draw desired garden features.

Even if your map shows the primary dimensions of your property, you'll need to take other measurements. This task will be easier if you use a fiberglass, nylon-clad steel, or chrome-steel measuring tape on a reel. These tapes, noted here in order from least to most expensive, come in longer lengths than the retractable type and are more suited to measuring larger spaces.

Combine Convenience and Aesthetics.

Although you want your property to be aesthetically pleasing, it should also be convenient to use. Try to keep human needs in mind. For example, while you're noting the paths and walkways, think about how convenient they are to use. Does the path follow a route that family members actually walk, or do they tend to cut corners and step through planting beds? Is the driveway wide enough, or do vehicles often drive off the edge, damaging adjacent lawn and plantings?

Sun and Shade Patterns

Knowing the light intensity at different locations on your property is extremely important when choosing plants. While a great variety of plants thrive in dappled sunlight or in shade where the light is fairly bright, your choice of plants is more limited for deeply shaded areas.

Patterns of sun and shade will change throughout each day and over the course of the year. Because the pattern of shadows is constantly shifting, it is important to record where the shady spots are at different times of the day and year. In the early morning and late afternoon, the sun will be low in the sky, casting long shadows. At noon, shadows will be short. During winter months, the sun remains low in the sky throughout the day, although a property with deciduous trees may receive more sunlight in winter, when the leaves have fallen, than in summer. The sun is high in the sky in summer, when its warmth and light intensity are increased.

It's not necessary to record the shadow cast by every structure on your property every minute of the day. But do make note of spots such as the north side of the house that are in deep shade for most of the day as well as other areas that may get only three or four hours of sunlight per day. Generally, the south side of the house will receive sunlight for most of the day.

Although shade is an important consideration, so too is sun. You may want to reserve the sunniest spots for a swimming pool or a vegetable garden. Also consider the time of day you are most likely to use such spaces. If you plan to sit outdoors in the sun after work, you won't want the patio on the east side of the house, which gets only morning sun. On the other hand, an eastern exposure is ideal for alfresco breakfasts.

Developing a Landscape Design

An ancient Roman maxim states, "It is a bad plan that admits of no modifications," and a plan for a landscape design illustrates this point perfectly. A good landscape design is the foundation upon which you will build for years to come. You'll likely make adjustments as time passes, but the basic structure of a well-designed landscape will help guide you.

Local Restrictions
Rules and regulations on issues such as fence height, pools, spotlights, decks, and other construction projects vary from community to

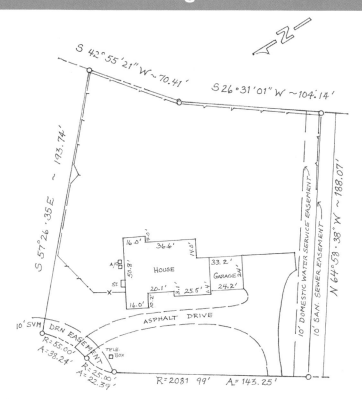

A plat map shows the precise boundaries, the measurements of the lot, and the position of the house, garage, and existing easements. Get one from the tax assessor's office.

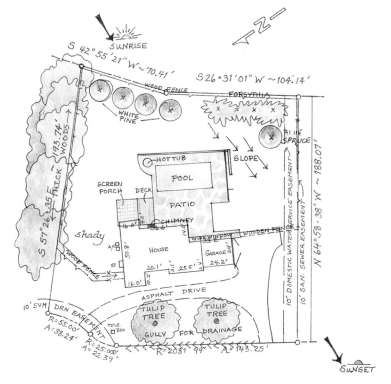

Completing a base map is an important first step in landscaping. Here the owner has indicated extensive information about his property and plans.

Useful Information

Gather all of the following information and add it to your Base Map before beginning the design process.

- Place Lot Boundaries, as described on page 8
- House Location, as described on page 8
- Locations of Other Structures, as described on page 8
- Underground Utilities, including electric cables, water pipes, sewer pipes, or a septic system
- Easements
- Overhead wires and heights
- Utility meters
- Air conditioner unit
- Slopes and water and/or melt-off drainage patterns
- Gutter downspouts
- Buried drainage pipes
- Puddle locations and sizes
- Eroded areas, if any
- Prevailing wind patterns
- Frost pockets
- Areas of intense sunlight and shade
- Lights and types
- Sprinklers and types
- Views, both desirable and undesirable
- Noisy areas
- Existing trees, gardens, plantings
- Any other useful information

Seasonal Shade

The sun and shade patterns change over the course of the year. In the winter, when the sun is low in the sky, the shadows cast by the deciduous tree and shrubs are longer than those cast in the summer sun.

community. Before you embark on any hardscape project, check with your local building authorities to learn whether permits are required and if any restrictions will apply.

If your property has any public rights-of-way or setbacks (areas along property boundaries where construction is prohibited), be sure you know their exact locations. Be aware that your property may not extend all the way to the public road. In many communities, the town or county may own as much as 20 feet of what may look like your property.

Ways to Visualize Your Plans

While a landscape map can give a good two-dimensional, top view of your property design, it doesn't give you the perspective that you have

Enlarge a photograph of your property that gives good perspective to help you visualize a landscape design. Cover the enlargement with a clear sheet of plastic, and use water-based markers to draw proposed garden features.

on foot. For this, you need what architects call a frontal elevation. It's a simple matter to create this view using a photograph.

Find a vantage point that gives you a good overview of your property. If your property is too wide to fit into one frame, shoot several photo prints and tape them together, or borrow a camera with a wide-angle lens. Request 4 x 6-inch prints or larger; then have a copy center make enlarged copies up to 11 x 17 inches.

A black-and-white photo or photocopy is an excellent means of assessing the strengths and weaknesses of an existing design. Without the distraction of color, you can better analyze the design in terms of form and texture.

Add New Features. Place a clear sheet of plastic over the photograph and draw on it with water-based markers. Plastic makes the use of different colored pens easier, giving a sense of form in your design as well as its colors. And it lets you easily erase.

As an alternative to plastic, tape a piece of tracing paper over the enlarged photocopy, and draw in the existing plantings and features

you plan to keep. Then draw in the new landscape elements you have in mind. It's not necessary to give an artistically accurate rendering of the plants. Simply capture the basic shapes, and draw them as close to scale as possible. Be sure to draw the plants at their mature size so that you can see how the design will look when it has grown, and can gauge how many plants you'll need. If you don't like the design, no problem: just try again with a new piece of tracing paper.

To give you a better sense of scale, it may help to position reference markers before you take the photograph. Place several 6-foot vertical stakes at different points on your property to serve as guides to height. When you draw in your plants, 3-foot plants will be half the height of the pole.

More Design Help

Today there's a wide selection of computer programs that allow you to experiment with plant combinations and move plants around easily without the effort of drawing and

redrawing on paper. Some of the programs include information on each plant's growing requirements. In others, you can input plants when they are young and small and then push a button to see how much they will grow in five years. The programs include predrawn mapping symbols for trees, shrubs, annuals, and perennials. There are even shapes and symbols that represent hardscape elements such as decks, stone walls, fences, and pools, and different textures to represent paving materials such as gravel, mulch, and brick.

If you'd prefer to arrange landscaping symbols with your hands rather than draw them or manipulate them on a computer, consider the various garden design books and kits that include grid paper and reusable, movable flower and plant images. The better products include plant lists with cultivation information, as well as valuable comments on regional differences. They also indicate how the plants will relate to one another by color, height, and bloom time, as well as by shape and texture of flower and leaf.

For a more hands-on approach, you can position stick-on trees, shrubs, and flowers with kits such as the one shown above. The "plants" come in different sizes and are scaled to fit the grids to which they adhere.

Computer-generated landscape design programs allow you to move plants around and try different designs almost effortlessly. The programs help you to visualize how a proposed design will actually look.

set the stage

Adding Structure

Once you've put your landscape design on paper, the next step is to lay the groundwork. This includes the soil and drainage; it may also include irrigation and lighting systems. Garden lighting and irrigation systems can be optional niceties, but good-quality soil and proper drainage are essential to success. While few people find preparation of the infrastructure as visually and emotionally satisfying as planting, these tasks are as important to a landscape as utilities are to a house.

Soil and Drainage. Good soil is essential for your plants to grow properly. For a garden to flourish with healthy plants that are strong enough to resist pests and diseases, you must first invest in improving the soil. Unless your property drains sufficiently so that rain water doesn't cause flooding or erosion, you may need to improve the drainage.

Irrigation. An irrigation system may be a seldom-needed convenience in regions that only occasionally experience extended dry periods. However, as droughts become more widespread, an irrigation system is almost essential unless you have lots of time to move the garden hose about. Often when a garden is hand-watered, some areas get more than enough water while other parts are slighted.

Lighting. Landscape lighting may seem like a luxury, but it can improve the security of your property, as well as making paths safer after dark. On warm evenings, it also extends the number of hours when you can enjoy your landscape. Throughout the year, a well-lit garden makes a dramatic backdrop to uncurtained windows after dark.

Examine the Soil

Unless you purchase a home where the previous owners were avid gardeners and worked the soil for some time, the odds are high that the quality of soil on your property is poor. Once you commit to improving the soil, have it analyzed to find out its pH level and nutrient content.

Soil is a living organism, and as with most organisms, it changes constantly. To keep abreast of any changes in pH and nutrient balance, you should test your soil every three to four years. The trouble and expense are small costs for the advantage of knowing exactly what nutrients or soil amendments your plants need.

Thorough preparation allows you to create the landscape that best suits your needs.

From properly prepared soil, healthy seedlings emerge and grow strong.

PH Effect on Plants

This chart suggests the importance of conducting a soil test before planting new trees or shrubs or attempting to chemically amend existing problems. For most plants, the ideal soil pH ranges from moderately acidic (5.5) to neutral (7.0). A low pH number (4.5 or lower) indicates high soil acidity; a high pH number (10.0 or higher) indicates high soil alkalinity. Relative acidity greatly affects the availability of nutrients to the plants.

The bar widths in this chart approximate the availability of essential nutrients at various pH levels; the narrower the bar width, the less available the nutrients. The first six elements are needed in larger amounts. Based on USDA charts showing the availability of nutrients in various kinds of soil, the chart represents only an approximation of nutrient availability in hypothetical "general" garden soil.

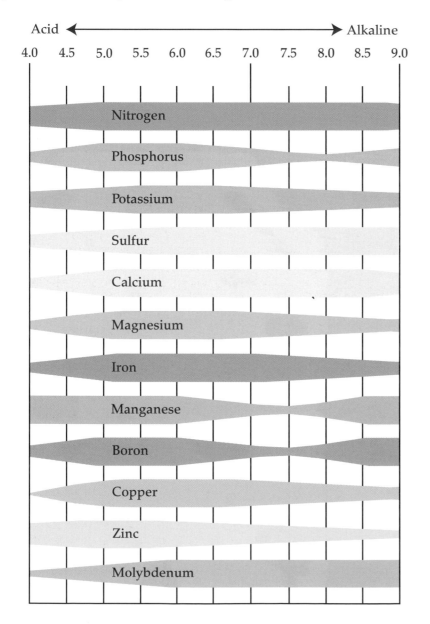

Soil Analysis

Cooperative Extension agents get many calls from people whose plants are ailing. Agent Patricia McAleer in Fairfax County, Virginia, says, "The first question they ask me is what spray should they use. Instead they should be asking if there is something wrong with the soil."

The basis of a healthy garden is its soil. Pests may annoy and diseases may intrude, but in most cases if the plants are growing in good soil, they will be resilient enough to overcome these travails. On the other hand, if the soil is missing a key nutrient or if the pH is off for a particular plant, the plant will begin to fail and will then be vulnerable to a host of pests and diseases.

pH Levels. The pH level is a measure of how much hydrogen is in the soil, which in turn affects how available nutrients are to your plants. Most ornamental plants, vegetables, and herbs do best in soil with a pH between 5 and 7. Woodland plants, including rhododendrons, azaleas, ferns, and astilbes do best in slightly acidic, or "sour," soil (below 5), while plants such as clematis prefer alkaline, or "sweet," soil with a pH of 8 or higher. Turf grass does best with a pH of 5.8 to 6.6. Soil pH figures are always given in a range. But, be aware that pH figures change exponentially. If your soil is at the extreme ends of the range or outside the suggested figure, you will most likely need to add amendments.

Most garden centers sell pH test kits with which you can test your own soil. However, for a nominal fee, the Cooperative Extension will measure the pH, and more importantly, give you a report indicating what, if anything, should be added to the soil and in what amounts. The Extension agent will determine whether the soil is sandy, clay, loam, or some combination of the three. This is important information because it affects the amounts and types of amendments needed.

Acidic and Alkaline Soil. Typically parts of the country that receive plenty of rain, such as the eastern third of the United States and Canada, tend to have acidic soil. Dry regions, such as the southwestern United States, usually have alkaline soil. However, don't assume that the soil on your property matches what is typical for the region. Parts of your property could have significantly different pH levels if the soil was heavily fertilized, if it's located at the end of a flood runoff, or if mineral substances ever leached into the soil. If you are new to the property, it's a good idea to bring in several samples from different parts of the property for analysis to obtain a complete picture of your soil.

Nutrient Analysis. A nutrient analysis requires serious chemistry. It's usually best to pay the fee for a soil analysis from your Cooperative Extension Service or from a commercial laboratory that includes information on soil pH as well as a breakdown of the soil's nutrients. The report will include recommendations on the amounts and types of amendments and fertilizers needed. Nitrogen is the one basic nutrient that usually isn't included because nitrogen levels in soil fluctuate daily, making that measurement meaningless.

Testing and Treating Lawns. Because lawns cover a large proportion of most properties, they are particularly important areas for soil testing. Although many people regularly lime their lawns, frequent applications of limestone may be unnecessary or even harmful to your grass. Save money by applying lime only when a soil test shows your lawn needs it. Grass needs a different balance of primary nutrients (nitrogen, phosphate, and potassium) than ornamental plants, so be sure to specify that the tested soil will be used for a lawn.

Excessive use of fertilizer is not only a waste of money, it disturbs the natural balance of microorganisms and makes lawns more prone to disease and thatch build-up. Plus the excess fertilizer may wash into water sources and pollute them. If you have a complete soil analysis done on your lawn every few years, you will know how much fertilizer to buy and whether the soil needs any additional lime. As a result, you will be able to make informed and environmentally responsible decisions about nutrients.

Taking a Soil Sample

The directions are the same whether you are measuring the pH or nutrient content. Indicate what you plan to grow because lawns, vegetables, and perennials have different pH requirements. Collect samples from several spots for an average reading. Mix the samples in a jar or plastic bag; allow the soil to thoroughly air-dry before testing it.

1. Dig Down 8 Inches. Bag the soil. Remove soil from several spots in one bed and mix them together.

2. Test the Soil with a Kit. Add the appropriate solution to a measured amount of the soil sample.

3. Shake the Solution. Cap the tube and shake it until the soil and solution are thoroughly blended.

4. Read the Results. Match the color of the resulting solution with the chart to determine the pH.

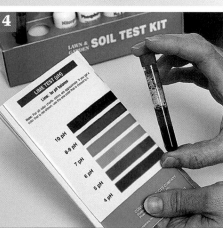

Understanding Soil Texture

In addition to having an appropriate pH and blend of nutrients, your soil should have a good structure, with spaces for air and water. Structure can be improved, although the texture—clay, sand, or loam—will not change.

Clay Soil. To determine the soil texture squeeze a handful in your palm. Heavy clay soil will form a tight ball. Clay is composed of extremely fine particles that pack together closely, so water drains slowly. Clay soil contains very little oxygen. Because it is dense, roots have a hard time pushing through.

Sandy Soil. Sandy soil, by contrast, will not hold together. Its loose, coarse particles allow space for lots of oxygen and easy root growth. Water can drain easily, but it can also leach out essential nutrients. Another disadvantage of sandy soil is that it dries out quickly.

Silty Soil. Silty soil feels silky or even soapy. Silt is sedimentary material that is coarser than clay but still composed of fine particles. It compacts easily.

Loam. The ideal soil is a rich loam balanced in its composition of clay, silt, and sand particles, and containing plenty of organic material such as humus or manure. When you squeeze loam in your hand, it will form a shape, but then crumble easily. Loam retains enough water for plant roots, but it still drains freely and is well aerated.

You can't change the texture of your soil, but by improving soil structure you can make any soil behave more like ideal loam. The easiest way to improve the structure of any soil is to add organic matter.

Organic matter lightens up heavy clay soil, improving drainage by creating more spaces for air and water. It also improves the structure of sandy soil by acting as a sponge to help hold water and nutrients so they aren't so easily washed away.

Amending any soil with organic materials brings its structure as close as possible to the ideal for growing plants, and at the same time enriches it with microorganisms that increase the soil's (and therefore your plants') health.

Soil Improvements

Soil Amendments

"Put a five-dollar plant into a ten-dollar hole" is common advice. If you've invested money in a plant, you'd better invest even more in creating an environment where it can grow and be healthy.

Soil scientists have identified about 4,000 species of beneficial microorganisms. These unseen creatures perform a host of valuable functions. Some convert nitrogen from the air into water-soluble compounds, making the nutrient available to plants. Others promote the decay process which transforms garden waste into nutrient-rich humus. There are microbes that feed on harmful plant pathogens and others that interact with plant roots to help them absorb mineral nutrients. Another group works to bind together the mineral particles in soil with the organic additions. Soil without these beneficial microorganisms is literally dead.

Once you've committed to amending the soil in at least a small area, the next step is to check the moisture content. Slightly moist soil is easiest to dig. If a handful feels moist and crumbles easily, you're ready to go. If the soil feels dry, water the ground

---

SMART TIP

Soil Texture

Soil texture is determined by the percentage of sand, silt, and clay. Sand particles can be as large as $\frac{1}{12}$ inch, while clay particles are as tiny as $\frac{1}{12,500}$ inch. However, most soil is a mixture of particle sizes and is described by the dominant material, as shown here. Loam is ideal garden soil with a combination of sand, silt, and clay.

Humus   Loam   Loamy Sand

Clay Loam   Silt Loam   Sandy Loam

Organic Amendments for Soil

Amendment	Significant Source of Organic Matter	Nutrients/Minerals Provided
Alfalfa Meal	Yes	Trace Minerals
Crab Meal		Nitrogen
Greensand		Potash, 32 Trace Minerals
Kelp Meal		Potash, Trace Minerals
Peat Moss	Yes	
Rock Phosphate		Phosphate, Calcium, Silicas, 11 Trace Minerals
Sul-Po-Mag		Potash, Magnesium
Manure	Yes	Many Nutrients
Worm Castings	Yes	11 Trace Minerals

Healthy soil is alive with beneficial organisms. In addition to worms, which till the soil as well as add nutrients in the form of their castings, loam is rich in microscopic life which performs a wealth of valuable functions for plants, including making nitrogen available and feeding on plant pathogens.

thoroughly and wait a couple of days. If the handful feels wet or leaves mud on your hands, wait a few days and retest. Soil structure can be severely damaged if you try to work wet soil.

Compost: The Best Soil Amendment

Compost is the result of a marvelous alchemy that transforms garden and kitchen waste into garden gold. When piled together for a period of time, everyday garden ingredients, including fallen leaves, garden trimmings, weeds, grass clippings, and kitchen scraps decompose into a crumbly black, organic material rich in earth-worms and healthy soil bacteria.

This free garden resource, often referred to as "black gold," is ideal for amending soil, topdressing lawns and beds instead of using chemical fertilizers, mulching beds, improving the texture and moisture-retentive properties of soil, and even using straight as a planting medium.

Use Compost to Improve Soil Texture. Compost loosens clay soil, improving its structure and tilth (workability) so that the soil is easy to cultivate and holds moisture well. In sandy soil, compost acts like a sponge to hold nutrients and water.

In any soil, compost supplies nutrients and beneficial microorganisms. Compost also brings the pH closer to neutral. Don't worry about overdosing the soil with organic amendments. You never can have too much.

Compost happens naturally. Walk through an old-growth forest and notice the spongy, rich soil under the trees, which is the result of centuries of decomposing leaves breaking down into humus. However, you can speed up the natural process. To

Compost breaks down fastest if you layer the "brown" and "green" material. The other ingredients for successful compost are air and water. Here the wire cage allows for ample air. Water your compost heap during periods of drought.

Create disposable compost bins with bales of straw. The straw will decompose along with the other garden waste, eventually contributing to the compost supply. These bins are based on a design by organic gardening specialist Elliot Coleman.

One pound of worms will turn a pound of kitchen waste into compost every day under average conditions. An outdoor wormery should be in a sheltered spot where temperatures do not fluctuate greatly. Worms thrive in temperatures ranging from 60° to 70°F.

A stone "river bed" is an attractive landscape feature, and is particularly useful to protect a slope from erosion when rain runoff is heavy. It is essentially an earthen ditch lined with stones.

This berm keeps water away from the house, channeling it toward the street. Without the berm running parallel to the hillside, water runoff down the slope would settle at the house foundation where it can create problems.

work most efficiently, the microorganisms that cause composting need a balanced diet of carbon and nitrogen as well as air and moisture.

Composting is easy. Anyone can create their own black gold regardless of the size of their garden. No fancy equipment or special expertise is needed. At the end of the season, you'll reap the rewards of finished compost, knowing that you made it all by yourself.

Containers for Composting

There are more than 100 composting bins currently on the market, as well as a lot of do-it-yourself designs such as suggestions for creating compartments with stacked cinder blocks or wire cages supported with stakes. While a specially designed bin may be useful, it is not essential. Don't let the lack of a container keep you from composting. Many gardeners successfully make

wheelbarrow-loads of compost simply by piling all the material directly on the ground.

Improving Drainage

Soil should be contoured to direct water away from the house foundation into storm drains. When builders construct a new house, they usually design for water runoff with downspouts, swales, and drainage ditches. However, you may need to add to the existing drainage plan to cope with the freak storms that drop enormous amounts of water in minutes, creating rivers down slopes. There are many kinds of drainage options, ranging from simple measures to elaborate underground systems that might include gravel-filled trenches or drain tiles. Because underground systems are so labor intensive, it's wise to search for the simplest solution.

If you plan major digging, you may need a permit from local building officials. Even if no permit is required, make certain you know the locations of underground lines for telephone, water, electricity, and so on. When digging trenches by hand, use a straight-edged spade, rather than a rounded shovel, so the walls of the trenches remain square. Also slope your trenches gently down hill at a rate of at least 1 inch per 8 feet. Several drainage options are described below.

Berms

A berm is a mound of earth that allows you to direct water away from the house or from an area that's vulnerable to erosion. In addition to directing water, a berm can serve as a lovely raised planter. Berms are also useful for creating privacy, for noise control, and to deflect winds.

Determine the approximate

amount of soil you will need for the berm, based on its length, width, and average height. Soil is sold by the cubic yard, which is 3 feet x 3 feet x 3 feet. Order soil by the truckload. Be sure to specify that you want land-scape-quality topsoil. When the dirt arrives, check it before they dump it. Topsoil should be dark, loose, and crumbly, not full of rocks or sticks. To avoid tire damage from the delivery truck, you may need to dump the load some distance from the berm site and haul the soil in a wheelbar-row. Grade the sides of the berm to a gentle slope. Then plant ground cov-ers, shrubs, or perennials so the roots will hold the new soil in place.

Swales and Drainage Ditches

A swale is simply a dip or depres-sion. A drainage ditch can route water from the swale away from your house. In some neighborhoods, the drainage ditch running along the

front of the property is concrete. Within residential properties, earthen ditches are often planted with grass or a ground cover to prevent erosion. If you already have such a ditch, you could transform it into an attractive "dry riverbed" by lining it with stones and edging it with plants that enjoy moist soil such as Louisiana iris, for-get-me-not, or meadow rue.

Catch Basins

Standing water and soggy soil in low spots often can be handled by catch basins. Purchase a ready-made catch basin, and install it under-ground at the lowest point where the water gathers. From the catch basin, dig a trench for a drainpipe that will funnel water away to a storm drain or an area where it can flow away prop-erly. Catch basins typically have a grate at soil level and a holding reservoir where water can collect before draining away through the pipe. Inside the basin is a sediment

trap that catches any leaves or debris. Remember to clean out the trap periodically so debris doesn't accumulate and block the drainpipe.

Dry Wells

If you don't have a storm drain or other convenient place to dispose of excess water, build a dry well at the lowest part of the area to be drained and run all the drain lines to it. A dry well holds excess water until the sur-rounding soil can absorb it. The size of the dry well will depend on the local rainfall. Dry wells 2 to 4 feet in diameter and 3 feet deep are gener-ally adequate in parts of the country with moderate rainfall, where it does not usually flood. Dig the hole, run the drainpipes into the hole, and fill the hole with gravel or rocks. Cover the hole with a concrete slab or other paving material, sod, or topsoil.

A catch basin can be installed at a low point in the garden where water settles. The collected water will flow through the pipe at the basin's bottom. The pipe should empty into a storm drain or an area where the water can disperse without causing damage.

A dry well is useful if you do not have storm drains to collect excess water. Direct drainpipes so they empty into a gravel-filled hole 2 to 4 feet in diame-ter and 3 feet deep. From there the water can disperse gradually through the surrounding soil. Cover a dry well with a concrete slab or other paving material, or lay sod on top as shown here.

This hillside is wasted landscape.

Bulldozer creates terraces.

Terraces add planting interest.

Flexible Drainpipes

Use flexible drainpipes to move runoff water away from structures and to channel it to areas where it can percolate into the earth or drain away. Dig a trench wide enough to accommodate the flexible pipe and about 1 foot deep. Be sure to make the trench slope (at least 1 inch for every 8 feet) so the water will run downhill away from its source. Lay the pipe in the trench, connecting it to downspouts with specially designed sleeves.

If you are using perforated pipe, line the bottom of the trench with 2 inches of gravel and lay the pipe on top with the holes facing down so they don't get clogged with dirt and debris. Fill in the trench with soil and cover with sod or backfill with gravel. Be sure to keep the exit end of the pipe open and clear so that water can escape freely. Direct it to a swale or to a spot where it can soak into the surronding soil. If you plant around the exit to disguise it, avoid blocking the water flow.

Grading Options

The reasons for grading range from aesthetic to utilitarian. You can add visual interest to your garden by varying the contours and levels, or make a dangerously steep slope easy to navigate by altering the grade. Always contact your local building department before embarking on any landscape construction project. And leave larger earth-moving jobs to a professional, such as a landscape architect or civil engineer. It's too easy to create flooded basements, or an accidental pond in a neighbor's yard.

Writing in her book *Rosemary Verey's Making of a Garden*, garden designer Rosemary Verey says, "If a client's garden is naturally flat, I wonder where and how a change of level can be created." She loves formal sunken gardens because they let you stand at the top and enjoy the pattern of the beds. If that is not practical, she recommends a raised bed, "to enable you to see the plants from a different viewpoint. Its retaining wall can be comfortable to sit on and gives the opportunity to use plants which love to cascade down."

A gentle slope is an opportunity to "present" plants; the slope raises successive plants slightly so they can be viewed from a perspective not possible on flat soil. A slope is also an ideal situation for a rock garden where small plants that would get lost in a larger environment can be showcased by tucking them next to attractive rocks.

This Japanese-style graded landscape divides a hill into two slopes. A simple bridge spans the slopes and leads to a stepping-stone path that follows the contours of the sloping ground.

Grading is often required for paved paths and patios. If your proposed patio site is near your house and is relatively flat, it's easy to create a level surface with a slight slope or grade that drains away from the house foundation. A slope of ¼ inch per foot is usually adequate. If the patio won't be near a structure, create a single central high point to avoid puddles.

Taming a Slope by Grading

Before it was graded, the large hill dotted with randomly-placed trees, opposite top left, was not a landscape asset. And the sloping lawn was a nuisance to mow. A small bulldozer was sufficient to move the earth to create two terraces connected by a steep slope and move the large trees to more logical places. The short, steep hill that remains after grading is ideal for a garden.

Building Hillside Terraces

These terraces were built so a vineyard and orchard could be planted on the sloping land. A home gardener built them in the spring when the ground was soft and the winter rains were finished. The northern California coastal soil was naturally porous with a gravel base; thus there were no drainage problems. The gardener does not recommend building such a terrace in clay soil without a retaining wall.

1. Choose the Location. Before the hillside was terraced, it was quite steep. But this area received the optimal sunlight for a vineyard and an orchard and had great potential. Some old hardwood trees block the wind.

2. Build the Terraces. Using a gas-powered tiller and a shovel, the homeowner built the terraces. It required many passes with the tiller, which cut just 8 inches at a time. Each terrace was 4 feet, half filled and half cut.

3. Seed the Terraces. Fast-germinating wildflower seeds were well-established plants when the winter rains began. Vegetables also held the soil until the vines and trees were established.

4. Plant the Saplings. Fruit trees were planted, and the homeowner hung wire between poles to support the grape vines. The wildflowers covered the terraces, and some reseeded themselves the following year.

Creating Terraces

Terracing a steep hillside is a time-honored way to transform unused land into broad level "steps" for garden beds or paved areas. If you want several terraces to traverse a slope, connect them with steps made of stone, pavers, or wood, depending on which material would look best in your overall design.

Some communities have regulations against homeowners building retaining walls more than 4 feet high. If your embankment requires a taller wall, either build a series of terraces with shorter retaining walls, or hire a professional engineer to design your wall and a contractor to build it. Many communities require landscape construction permits for walls 3 feet or taller, so be sure to check with your local building inspector before you begin building.

Even well-packed soil is not completely stable on a slope. If you need to do extensive grading to create your terraces, contact a soil engineer or landscape architect to ensure that the final terracing will be structurally sound. If you plan to attack the project without professional help, begin at the bottom, just below the slope. Build a retaining wall on ground that is already level. Use the soil from the low end of the slope near the wall to backfill the gap between the wall and the slope until you have created a level terrace. Continue until you have created the number of terraces you want. It is essential to provide drainage for a retaining wall so water doesn't build up behind it. Either build weep holes in the wall, or run perforated drainpipe behind the wall before you backfill with soil.

Materials for retaining walls include wood, stone, precast blocks, and concrete. Choose a building material that is suitable for the site and that creates the overall effect you want. Details for constructing wooden retaining walls are given with the illustration below.

Building Wooden Retaining Walls

Wooden retaining walls are generally the easiest and least expensive way to tame a slope; they usually look less formal than terraces walled with stone or brick. Wood tends to survive longer in drier climates than wet ones and on well-drained slopes. On a large slope, where the wall must support tons of earth, you must use heavy lumber such as landscape timbers. To delay rotting, choose either pressure-treated lumber or wood that is resistant to decay, such as redwood, cedar, or cypress. If you want to avoid digging deep holes for support posts, you can use deadman braces to give structural strength to a timber retaining wall. Deadmen should be installed along your wall in the second or third course from the bottom and in the second course from the top.

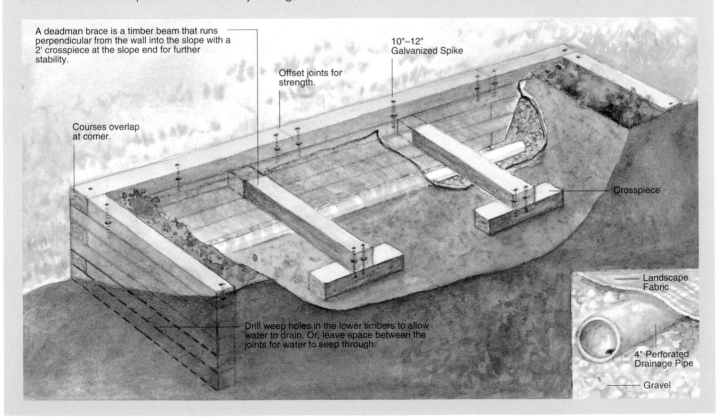

A deadman brace is a timber beam that runs perpendicular from the wall into the slope with a 2' crosspiece at the slope end for further stability.

Offset joints for strength.

10"–12" Galvanized Spike

Courses overlap at corner.

Crosspiece

Landscape Fabric

4" Perforated Drainage Pipe

Gravel

Drill weep holes in the lower timbers to allow water to drain. Or, leave space between the joints for water to seep through.

Recommended Trees and Shrubs for Poor Soil

Intense soil amendment is particularly important if you are planting perennials, annuals, or vegetables. If you are planting trees and shrubs, which have root systems that will delve far deeper than you can amend, your best bet is to choose plants that are adapted to the native soil. Below are lists of trees and shrubs that are proven performers in specific soils.

Clay Soil

Trees
- *Alnus glutinosa* (common alder), Zones 4–7
- *Cedrus libani* ssp. *atlantica* (Atlas cedar), Zones 7–9
- *Cryptomeria japonica* (Japanese cedar), Zones 6–9
- *Fraxinus species* (ash), zones vary with species
- *Juglans nigra* (eastern black walnut), Zones 5–9
- *Lagerstroemia indica* (crape myrtle), Zones 7–10
- *Metasequoia glyptostroboides* (dawn redwood), Zones 5–10
- *Oxydendrum arboreum* (sourwood), Zones 5–9
- *Populus species* (poplar), zones vary with species
- *Quercus palustris* (pin oak), Zones 5–8
- *Quercus robur* (English oak), Zones 5–8
- *Salix* x *sepulcralis* var. *chrysocoma* (golden weeping willow), Zones 4–9
- *Salix matsudana* 'Tortuosa' (contorted willow), Zones 5–8
- *Salix purpurea* (purple osier), Zones 4–9
- *Sambucus racemosa* (red-berried elder), Zones 4–7
- *Taxodium distichum* (bald cypress), Zones 5–10

Shrubs
- *Aronia arbutifolia* (red chokeberry), Zones 4–8
- *Calycanthus floridus* (Carolina allspice), Zones 5–9
- *Cornus alba* 'Sibirica' (red-barked dogwood), Zones 2–8
- *Cotoneaster species,* Zones 5–9
- *Kalmia latifolia* (mountain laurel), Zones 5–9
- *Ledum groenlandicum* (Labrador tea), Zones 2–6
- *Magnolia virginiana* (sweet bay), Zones 6–9
- *Photinia serratifolia* (Chinese photinia), Zones 7–9
- *Pyracantha species* (firethorn), Zones 6–10
- *Viburnum lentago* (sheepberry), Zones 3–8
- *Viburnum opulus* (European cranberry), Zones 4–8

Sandy Soil

Trees
- *Abies grandis* (grand fir), Zones 7–9
- *Acacia dealbata* (silver wattle), Zones 9–10
- *Acer negundo* (box elder), Zones 3–9
- *Betula pendula* 'Dalecarlica' (cutleaf European birch), Zones 3–8
- *Castanea sativa* (Spanish chestnut), Zones 5–8
- *Celtis australis* (European hackberry), Zones 6–9
- *Cupressus leylandii* (Leyland cypress), Zones 6–9
- *Eucalyptus ficifolia* (red-flowering gum), Zones 9–10
- *Gleditsia triacanthos* (honey locust), Zones 5–9
- *Phoenix canariensis* (Canary Island date palm), Zones 9–10
- *Pinus pinaster* (cluster pine), Zones 7–9
- *Pinus radiata* (Monterey pine), Zones 7–9
- *Pseudotsuga menziesii* ssp. *glauca* (Rocky Mountain Douglas fir), Zones 5–7
- Quercus ilex (holly oak), Zones 7–9
- *Schinus molle* (California pepper tree), Zones 9–10

Shrubs
- Acanthus spinosus (spiny bear's breech), Zones 5–9
- Calluna vulgaris (Scotch heather), Zones 5–7
- Cercis siliquastrum (Judas tree), Zones 8–9
- *Cistus* species (rock rose), Zones 7–10
- *Cytisus scoparius* (Scotch broom), Zones 6–9
- *Genista tinctoria* (dyer's greenweed) Zones 2–8
- *Juniperus* species (juniper), zones vary with species
- *Rosa pimpinellifolia* (Scotch rose), Zones 4–9
- *Spartium junceum* (Spanish broom), Zones 7–10
- *Yucca gloriosa* (Spanish dagger), Zones 7–10

Providing Irrigation

Although hand watering can be a relaxing, therapeutic occupation, it is time consuming. Except for plants growing in containers, it's almost impossible to give plants the thorough soaking they need with just a watering can. Portable sprinklers do a better job and take less hands-on time, but they require that you remember to move them at regular intervals.

To save hours of hand watering and dragging hoses, consider installing systems that drip water directly into the soil, or sprinkle water through the air. If you include automatic timers with your system, you can ensure that your plants consistently receive the amount of water they need.

Installing your own irrigation system is a great do-it-yourself project: challenging enough to give a sense of accomplishment when the job is done, but not so complicated that it takes a professional to do it right. In addition, the savings are significant. You can save 50 percent or more from the cost of a professional installation, and the time you spend on the project is minimal compared with the time you'd otherwise spend watering by hand over the years.

Drip Irrigation Systems

Drip irrigation is more versatile and flexible than sprinklers for most situations, other than lawns and ground covers. Drip irrigation delivers water at a slow rate directly to root systems. The long, slow delivery ensures that plants are deeply watered, even in clay soil where water absorption is slow.

With drip irrigation, there is no waste due to runoff and evaporation, and the deep watering encourages plants to grow deeper roots, making them more drought-tolerant. Because drip irrigation doesn't wet the foliage, plants are less likely to suffer from diseases resulting from damp foliage (which encourages some fungi), or from pathogens carried from upper leaves to lower ones in descending water droplets. Drip irrigation also reduces the need for pesticides, because damp leaves harbor some pests. Because the water is applied exactly where it is needed through custom-made emitters (holes) located only where you want water dispensed, weed plants have a harder time getting their share. In addition, drip lines do not need to be buried. Thus you can move the lines around easily and adapt your system to any changes you make in your garden design. It is easy to add new lines, remove old ones, or plug the holes for old feeder lines that are no longer required.

Planning Drip Systems. Starting with a base map of your property that shows the location of buildings, walkways, patios, water sources, and a layout of your garden beds and plants, divide your garden into zones based on the types of plants and their watering needs. For example, plants growing in shade would be one zone, trees and shrubs in another, the vegetable garden a third zone, and containers and hanging baskets in yet another zone. Annuals, which require frequent shallow watering, should be in a different zone from trees and shrubs that require infrequent but deep watering. Ideally each zone should have a separate drip watering circuit that is connected to its own valve.

The kind of soil you have will be a factor in determining the rate of flow you want from each emitter (water delivery device), and how many emitters you will need. Because heavy clay soil absorbs water slowly, you will want long, slow water delivery and therefore fewer emitters. Because sandy soil soaks up water quickly, allowing water to drain straight down, you'll need more emitters spaced closely.

A drip irrigation system is ideal for vegetable beds because the layout can be revised and amended as needed with each new crop. Set out the lines when the plants are young, and in a few weeks they will be completely hidden by the growing produce.

Materials. Supplies you will need for drip systems include ½-inch polyethylene hose (sufficient length to complete your design), hose fittings, an anti-siphon control valve for each watering zone, a pressure regulator, a filter to keep pipe debris from clogging the emitters, Y-filters to enable you to fertilize as you water, end caps, transfer barbs for extending lateral lines, polyethylene microtubing (the spaghetti-like lines that take the water from the main hose to the plants), and emitters.

Although not essential, an automatic timer is a real asset. Drip systems run for hours at a time, making it easy to forget that the water is running. With a timer, you don't have to remember to shut off the water. In the case of a large fruit or ornamental tree with a canopy spread of 15 feet in diameter, you should plan for six emitters. Smaller trees and shrubs require one emitter for every 2½ feet of canopy diameter.

Watering Table

Type of Plant	Water Needed Gallons per Week	Watering Frequency per Week		
		Moderate	Hot	Cool
Vines & Shrubs (2–3')	7	2	3	1–2
Trees & Shrubs (3–6')	10–15	2	3	1–2
Trees & Shrubs (6–10')	30–40	2	3	1–2
Trees & Shrubs (10–20')	100–140	2	3	1–2
Mature Trees (Over 20')	160–240	2	3	1–2
Flowers, Plants, Vegetables	3	2	3	1–2
Potted Plants	¾	2	3	1–2
Rows of Flowers or Vegetables	6	2	3	1–2

SMART TIP

Plan your drip irrigation system by dividing your plants into groups or zones based on their water requirements. Here, large trees that require deep, infrequent watering are on one line, the vegetable garden is a zone of its own, the flower beds are grouped together, and the containers have a separate system with drip lines running to each pot. Such a map is also useful for underground sprinklers with which you can water all of these plants plus lawns, but not containers. Also separate out plants growing in full sun, which will dry out faster than plants growing in shady areas.

Drip Watering Zones
- Trees & Shrubs
- Vegetable Gardens
- Container Plants
- Flower Beds & Ground Covers

Make a shopping list of all the supplies you will need to complete the system. Use the parts lists available from the manufacturers as a guide.

Installing Drip Systems. You can either bury the lines—being careful to keep the ends of the microtubing aboveground, cover them with mulch, or leave them above the ground. In annual and vegetable beds, the growing plants will soon hide most, if not all, of the aboveground tubing.

Maintenance. Sediment present in your tap water will accumulate in the irrigation lines and clog them. Every four to six months flush out the lines by opening the end caps and allowing water to run freely through the system for a few minutes. Also flush out the lines if they haven't been used for several months.

Filters should be checked monthly. Wash them under running water,

checking for tears or other damage; replace any that are damaged. Y-filters need less regular maintenance. They handle up to 720 gallons per hour (gph) through a screen.

Every few months check the emitters to make sure they are working properly. Also check an emitter if you notice that a nearby plant is wilting, or an unusual wetting pattern. Clean any emitters that have become clogged, and replace damaged ones.

If a line is damaged, repair it with a slip-on coupling. In areas with winter freezes, drain the lines and shut off the system before the first major frost. You also should protect the control head from freezing. The best way to do this is to install the control head with a union on either side of it. When the weather turns cold, just unbolt the control head and store it indoors until spring. Wrap it so rodents can't get to it over the winter.

Underground Sprinkler Systems

These irrigation systems involve buried pipes with sprinkler heads placed at regular intervals. Sprinklers spray water over the plants, wetting them the same way that rain does, at a rate as high as 9 gallons per minute. Sprinkler systems tend to work better for lawns and ground covers than for garden beds.

Planning Your Underground Sprinkler System. Excellent brochures by the major sprinkler companies give detailed step-by-step instructions for designing and installing their own sprinkler systems.

In addition, some of the larger companies will create a custom design for your property free of charge. Call their hotlines if you need help or have questions.

Use a copy of the landscape base map you created earlier to work out

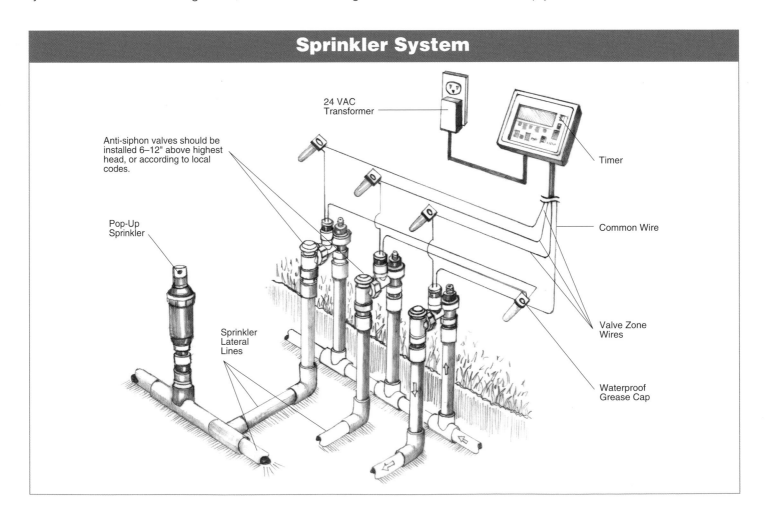

Sprinkler System

24 VAC Transformer

Timer

Anti-siphon valves should be installed 6–12" above highest head, or according to local codes.

Pop-Up Sprinkler

Sprinkler Lateral Lines

Common Wire

Valve Zone Wires

Waterproof Grease Cap

and draw your sprinkler system's design. If you haven't yet created a base map of your property, as explained in the previous chapter, draw your property to scale on a piece of graph paper. Then indicate the location of your water meter and the location and length of the service line to your house. If your water supply comes from a well, rather than from the city water supply, show where the well and pump are located.

Drip Irrigation Installation

Drip systems are fun to design and easy to install. You don't need wrenches, saws, or glue, and if you make a mistake, it is simple and inexpensive to remedy. Drip lines can be installed aboveground or below ground, and the design can be expanded or relocated as your needs evolve.

1. Measure the Tubing. Lay out the line; measure carefully; and cut it to the proper length. This system is designed to water containers. The tubing becomes round when it is filled with water.

2. Connect the Tubing at T-Joints. These joints connect several lines to a single water source. Punch holes where you want the emitters. These holes can be plugged and new ones punched as the garden changes.

Companies that manufacture drip irrigation supplies provide free brochures that give detailed instructions for designing and installing the systems. You can purchase kits with complete instructions for specific applications such as containers, vegetable gardens, and general landscape areas. Following is a summary of the usual steps.

3. Attach a Filter to the Water Source. Filters vary in size from very fine mesh to trap tiny particles to larger mesh openings. The sediment content of your water supply will dictate the type of filtering system necessary.

4. Set a Timer. The easiest way to run a drip irrigation system is to put everything on an automatic timer, which will turn the water on and off at custom intervals. The duration of each watering can also be programmed.

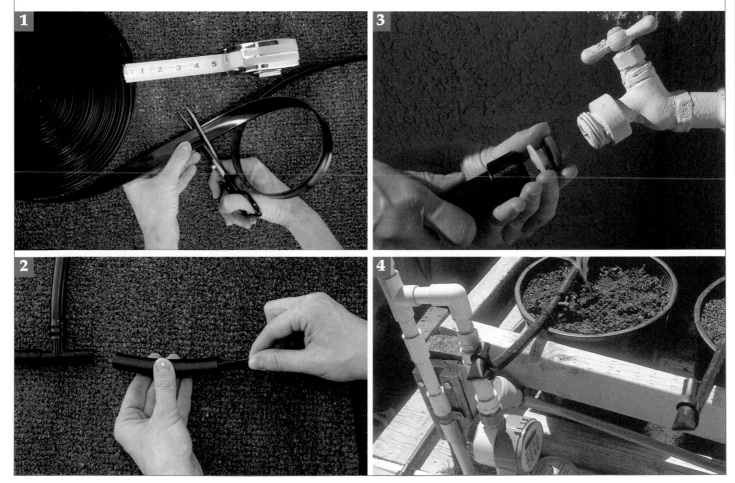

Well-placed lights along this waterside garden path encourage an evening stroll, and add a sense of enchantment to the lovely scene.

Outdoor Lighting

Ever-changing light transforms a garden's appearance throughout the day. A garden can look etched in sharp clarity in the bright sun of high noon. Bathed in the long, golden glow of the waning evening sun, the same garden can take on a rosy gilt. In early morning, when the sun shines through a mist, there's an ethereal, silvery quality to a garden's appearance. Come dusk, an unlit garden recedes and then disappears as twilight fades to night.

Outdoor lighting can transform night into an enchanting time, highlighting parts of the garden in new ways. Garden lights also prolong the time you can be outdoors, especially in the transition seasons of spring and autumn when the days are shorter but the temperature is still warm enough to be outdoors. Dining outdoors in the summer and lingering at the table late into the evening are added pleasures when your surroundings are bathed in soft light, perhaps occasionally punctuated by a dramatically uplit plant.

In addition to the aesthetic benefits, outdoor lighting can make your property safer both for walking and as a deterrent to burglars. To do its job, however, safety lighting must be installed properly. For example, a spotlight focused on the bottom of a set of steps or at a sharp change in a path may increase the hazard for a person moving from intense light into total darkness. A more general floodlighting is safer. Better yet, and more attractive, is a series of tier lights along a path or stairway, focusing light downward in even pools.

Burglars and prowlers tend to avoid well-lit properties, but all-night lighting wastes electricity. Rather than leaving lights on all night, you can install floodlight fixtures with sensors that respond to movement by switching the lights on for a preset number of minutes. One disadvantage of motion lights is that they also switch on when neighborhood pets pass through or when breezes move tree branches or other plants that are growing within range of the motion detectors.

Installing a 120-volt garden lighting system is an expensive and labor-intensive job that requires buried waterproof pipes. As with other electrical projects, strict safety codes must be followed. Installation of a 120-volt system is usually best left to professional electricians.

Fortunately, there is an inexpensive alternative to 120-volt systems, called low-voltage outdoor lighting. Low-voltage systems use only 12 volts of electricity instead of 120. A typical six-light set uses less electricity than a 60-watt bulb, costing pennies per evening to operate. Best of all, most of the low-voltage systems are reasonably inexpensive and easy to install.

Landscape lighting transforms a garden after dark from a black hole to a magical place where fascinating shapes and silhouettes are highlighted

Decorating With Lights

The two basic types of lighting are spotlighting and floodlighting. A spotlight is focused so the light beam strikes a defined area, creating a distinct line between the lit and unlit areas. A floodlight is more diffuse; it covers a wide general area with a gradual decline from well-lit to dark. In either case, the light can be intense or subdued, although in low-voltage systems the floodlighting is less bright than with 120-volt systems. Halogen bulbs produce the brightest light for low-voltage fixtures.

By positioning and combining spotlights and floodlights, you can create a wide variety of decorative lighting effects. It's often a good idea to experiment with portable lights to work out the effects you want, and then study a product list to determine which fixtures will produce those effects. The wiring for lights installed in trees can be vulnerable to falling branches, so secure the wire to the trunk of the tree to prevent problems. If you are using 120-volt lighting, run the wire up the tree trunk in a conduit that meets local building codes and is firmly attached to the tree.

Part of the art of designing is creating contrast. To be artistically effective, light should be complemented by shadow. Of course, you could floodlight your entire property so everything is as clearly seen as in the daylight; but your night garden will be more special, more mysterious, if you contrast lit areas with darker places. Change also adds interest to designs. With a low-voltage system, you can easily move lights around throughout the year. Highlight the blooming azaleas in spring, and then move the lights to showcase a summertime display elsewhere.

Avoid going overboard with colored lenses or bulbs. Yellow colored lights can be useful near a patio or outdoor sitting area because they attract fewer flying insects. In general, however, you'll be more pleased with white lights, which enhance the natural colors of the plants.

Low-Voltage Light Installation

The only hard part of installing low-voltage lights is deciding where to put them and what effects you want to create. Kits for specific purposes are available. Check them out to help you make your decisions. Try to minimize the amount of wire you need. Once you're ready to connect the wires, the job literally takes minutes.

Lay out the wire in a direct route and follow the manufacturer's instructions. Be careful not to exceed the prescribed number of lights for each circuit. Plug the transformer box into a properly installed outdoor outlet. If you don't have an outdoor outlet, have one installed by a professional electrician following local codes.

1. Connect the Wire Cable to the Transformer Box. Wrap the wire around the terminal screws. For proper connection, make sure the wire insulation is clear of the pressure plates. Tighten the screws firmly, and plug the box into a grounded outlet.

2. Connect the Lamps to the Low-Voltage Cable. Pinch the fast-lock connector, which is attached to the cable that runs from the light, onto the main line. You can undo the connection and move it at any time. The hole is tiny and the voltage is low, so there is no hazard.

3. Hide the Wires. Preinstalled wires run through the light fixture and are connected to the main line. You can bury the cable lines underground. But if you think you may be moving the system, the lines are perfectly safe left aboveground.

4. Position the Lamp. Anchor the lamp in place by pressing the lamp stake into the ground. In climates where heavy winter freezes cause heaving, dig a hole 8 inches deep and 6 inches wide for the lamp stake, and backfill the hole with gravel.

walls & fences

Vertical Elements

Landscape designs often benefit from vertical elements such as walls, fences, arches, arbors, pergolas, and decorative freestanding plant supports. Walls and fences help define boundaries as well as enclose special spaces. Properly positioned, an arbor or arch is an eye-catching accent, adding visual drama to the scene and providing an attractive focal point or point of passage between two parts of the garden. A pergola transforms an ordinary path into a special, shaded, and sheltered passageway, while a freestanding plant support is like an exclamation point, drawing attention to itself and creating a pleasant focus.

As an added bonus, any one of these features provides an opportunity to grow and enjoy the wide range of climbing plants such as clematis, wisteria, climbing roses, honeysuckle, trumpet vine, and jasmine. These vertical plants add a sense of lushness to the garden as they scramble up walls and over trellised arches or droop heavy panicles of flowers through the open fretwork ceiling of a pergola.

Arbors and other vertical structures work well when they serve as transitions between areas of the yard. They also provide a base for climbing plants.

Designing Walls

Walls impart a sense of permanence to a garden. They also provide structure, define boundaries, give privacy, and create pleasing microclimates. If designed to hold back earth, as when a slope is carved into level terraces, they are called retaining walls. A wall facing south will absorb and then radiate heat, jump-starting nearby plants' growth in spring and extending the growing season well into autumn. Walls also deflect the wind, adding protection as well as warmth. Walls make a wonderful backdrop to perennial borders; they have an advantage over hedges because plants don't have to compete for root space and nutrients as they do near a hedge. On the negative side, walls

built on the south end of a garden may block the light, and on a windy site they can create strange wind patterns. Despite these potential drawbacks, a wall is a valuable garden feature.

Building a freestanding wall up to 3 feet tall is an appropriate do-it-yourself project. If you need a taller structure, it is best to turn to a professional. You should also check with the local building inspector for restrictions on wall height. In addition to being a beautiful architectural feature, a wall must be designed for stability, and a freestanding wall must be able to remain upright in high winds. It takes experience and training to successfully construct a tall, strong wall.

Maintain Structural Integrity

The ratio of wall thickness to height determines structural soundness. Let a professional reinforce walls over 3 feet with internal rods or support pilasters. The foundation must be substantial to keep the wall from shifting due to settling and frost heaving. The necessary width and depth of the foundation depends on the soil's stability, the frost line (with the foundation extending below the lowest depth to which the soil freezes), and the wall's width. In stiff clay the foundation should be a minimum of 2 feet deep; in sand it should extend at least 3 feet into the soil. Generally the foundation should be twice as wide as the walls' thickness.

Constructing a Brick Wall

In addition to selecting brick, you must decide on the arrangement of bricks in the wall, called the bond. The four standard choices are running bond, stack bond, Flemish bond, and English bond. The bond patterns in which perpendicular mortar joints are bridged by courses above and below are generally stronger. Hence the weakest bond is the stack bond, although it should be fine to use for a low wall no more than 3 feet tall. Flemish and English bond, which have periodic headers that bind the double row of bricks, or wythes, are the strongest of the group.

Running Bond

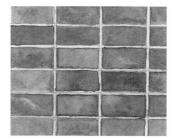

Stack Bond

Flemish Bond

English Bond

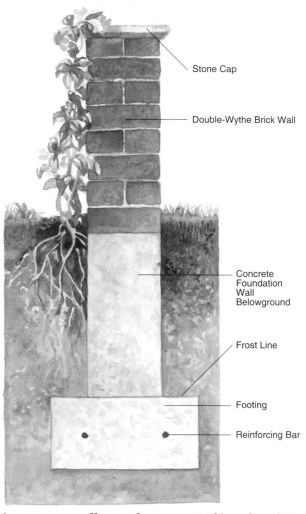

Stone Cap

Double-Wythe Brick Wall

Concrete Foundation Wall Belowground

Frost Line

Footing

Reinforcing Bar

A masonry wall must be supported by a foundation, including a footing that reaches below the frost line. A brick wall is like the tip of an iceberg. The footing should be twice the width of the wall and nearly as tall as the width.

Terminology

- **Bat:** A brick cut in half lengthwise.
- **Bed Joint:** A horizontal masonry joint.
- **Bond:** The arrangement of bricks in a wall that creates a pattern.
- **Collar Joint:** The vertical joint between wythes.
- **Course:** A horizontal row of bricks.
- **Footing:** A concrete foundation below the frost line to support walls.
- **Headers:** Bricks turned horizontally to the stretcher courses.
- **Head Joint:** A vertical masonry joint.
- **Jointing:** The finish given to the mortar that exudes from each course of bricks.
- **Pointing:** Repairing the joints of a wall.
- **Reinforcing Bar:** A steel rod used to reinforce concrete, both horizontally and vertically.
- **Sailor:** An upright brick with the broad face positioned out.
- **Soap:** A brick halved in width.
- **Soldier:** An upright brick with the narrow edge positioned out.
- **Split:** A brick halved in height.
- **Stretchers:** Bricks laid horizontally in the direction of the wall.
- **Wythe:** A vertical tier of bricks in a wall.

Decorative Features Add Stability.
Many of the decorative features in the design of a wall, such as a varied brick pattern (called the bond), an attractive cap or coping, and regularly spaced thicker wall sections called pilasters or piles are, in fact, incorporated to improve the structural integrity of the wall. The cap keeps water out of the wall, preventing the problem of expansion and contraction caused by freezing and thawing water caught in the seams. Aware of the importance of a coping or cap, Thomas Jefferson had the message, "If you keep my hat on I will last forever," carved on a stone wall he built in southern Virginia.

Open Walls Look Lighter. Not all walls are solid. Screen walls, made either by alternating bricks with open spaces or by using screen blocks, have an open, fretwork design that is visually less domineering than a solid wall. They are popular in hot southern climates because they allow cooling breezes to flow into the garden.

Open screen designs are usually set into a solid wall as a decorative element. They usually run between pilasters and begin several feet up from the ground atop a solid base of wall.

Whether you choose to build a wall yourself or hire an expert, be sure to check with your community's building inspector. You need to be in compliance with local ordinances regarding issues such as the height of the wall, type and depth of the foundation and footing, and any internal reinforcing rods that may be required.

Brick Walls

Brick is a classic material for garden walls. The warm tones of natural brick blend beautifully with buildings, plants, and surrounding soil. Brick adapts easily to many settings, and the standard-size blocks lend themselves to many design patterns and compositions. For the most part, the crisp edges and uniform mortar joints tend to give a brick wall a

formal feel. But you can be as creative in designing a brick wall as you can working with children's building blocks.

If you decide to build a brick wall, first study photographs to see the wide scope of possibilities for wall detailing and design. This wall will be a major investment, and you want to make sure you are completely satisfied with the final product.

There are three grades of brick suitable for outdoor walls. The cheapest bricks, which are made for general-purpose building, are called commons. Because they have no finish, they are subject to weathering. The next grade is called facing brick because there is a weather-resistant finish on the sides, or faces. This provides some resistance to weathering if the brick is laid with the finished facing exposed. The top grade of brick is called engineering brick. These bricks are the hardest and most impervious to weathering. Within these categories you can find bricks of different sizes and colors.

This low brick retaining wall doubles as an attractive raised planter. In addition to solving the problem of poor soil, a raised planter is easy to tend because you can sit on the edge of the wall, rather than having to work on your knees.

Stone Walls

Stone walls are beautiful landscape features, especially if they are made from native stone.

There are two types of stone used for building walls. *Rubble stone*, including fieldstone, is irregular in size and shape. *Ashlar* is stone that has been cut at the quarry to produce smooth, flat surfaces that stack easily.

The dry-laid stone walls that crisscross the New England countryside are made from local fieldstone that was picked out of the fields and put to good use. Walls made from quarried and cut ashlar stones are more formal looking and generally easier to build.

Whether you buy rubble or ashlar stone, it will be sold by the cubic yard at quarries and stone suppliers. Because of the extreme weight, ask your supplier to deliver it.

Determine the Amount of Stone. To work out how much stone you need for a dry-laid or mortared wall, multiply the length times the height times the width of your wall in feet to determine the cubic feet. To translate the resulting number into cubic yards, divide by 27. Add about 10 percent to your order if you are working with ashlar stone to allow for breakage and waste. If you are planning a rubble wall, add at least 25 percent.

Designing Retaining Walls

Masonry Retaining Walls

Retaining walls have a double purpose. They are ornamental, and they hold back soil to convert a slope into level areas or terraces.

Brick and Concrete Retaining Walls. Retaining walls of brick, concrete block, or poured concrete are usually reinforced with steel rebar. Well-made mortared masonry walls tend to be the strongest of all the types of retaining walls. Opt for these materials if your wall will be taller than 4 feet or if you are retaining an especially steep slope with unstable soil. Before you begin building, check with local authorities. Many communities require that you hire a professional engineer to design any retaining wall more than 4 feet tall.

Retaining walls constructed of brick or block must stand on a concrete footing to make them stable. Because retaining walls must be able to support the added weight of tons of soil, they must be even more stable than freestanding garden walls. As with garden walls,

Brick Retaining Wall Anatomy

Retaining walls must be very strong to hold back the tons of soil pushing against them. Waterlogged soil is even heavier and more unstable, so be sure to provide drainage behind the wall to remove excess water.

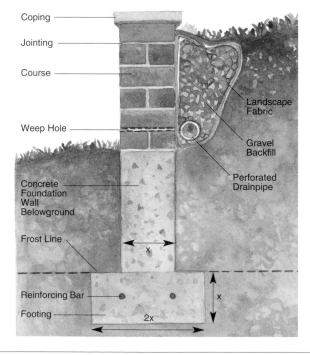

- Coping
- Jointing
- Course
- Weep Hole
- Concrete Foundation Wall Belowground
- Frost Line
- Reinforcing Bar
- Footing
- Landscape Fabric
- Gravel Backfill
- Perforated Drainpipe
- x
- 2x

The flat-topped gray stone wall makes a beautiful backdrop for the colorful annuals planted against it. The narrow planting bed, about the same depth as the wall is high, is in pleasing proportion to the wall.

To create a series of level terraces on a slope, use the soil from the base of the retaining wall as the backfill behind the wall, as seen in the top illustration. If you prefer one large, level space, cut the slope where you want the wall, and then use the excess soil to level the slope farther downhill, as shown in the bottom illustration.

the footing of retaining walls should extend below the frost line where freezing is an issue. Footings should be the same thickness as the wall and twice as wide as they are thick. For example, a brick wall 8 inches wide should be built on a footing that is 8 inches thick and 16 inches wide. (See drawing opposite.) In cases where the frost line runs from several inches to several feet below ground level, you can save on expensive wall materials by building a belowground wall of concrete on top of the footing, and then building the retaining wall on top of the concrete wall at ground level.

Build in Drainage. To ensure proper drainage (important for the stability of the wall, as well as for plant health), lay a perforated drainpipe behind the wall at the original ground level. If the drainpipe holes are on only one side of the pipe, be sure they face downward. Make sure the pipe slopes at least ¼-inch per foot to

ensure that it moves the water away from the wall instead of just collecting behind it. Surround the pipe with gravel to keep soil out of the pipe, and then backfill. Another option is to insert drainpipes through the lower part of the retaining wall every 32 inches so water can flow out the front of the wall.

Mortared Stone Retaining Walls

A mortared stone wall is no more durable than a dry-laid wall. (If it is properly built, a dry stone wall will endure for centuries.) However, mortared stone walls have a more formal look suitable for tailored gardens. A mortared wall also is preferable in situations where people are likely to disturb stones, perhaps by sitting or walking on the wall. A mortared stone wall can also be built with irregularly shaped stones, rather than those that fit snugly, because they'll be bonded together with mortar.

Footings are Required. Like brick walls, a mortared stone wall must stand on a footing with a depth equal to the thickness of the wall and a width twice the wall's thickness. Check with your local authorities on recommendations and regulations regarding the underground depth of the footing to accommodate frost lines.

Begin with the largest stones on the bottom course. The squarest stones are most suitable for the ends and corners of the wall, and the flattest stones are best on top. If your wall will be built with different-sized stones running in parallel rows, be sure to use bond stones that extend through the full thickness of the wall every few feet. Stagger the placement of the bond stones in each course so that they are never directly above one another.

Building Dry-Laid Stone Retaining Wall

Retaining walls must stand on a firm footing. Excavate a trench down about 6 inches and tamp the dirt, leaving an undisturbed base on which to build the wall. Line the trench with landscape fabric. Put a few inches of gravel on top of the fabric, rake it level, and then lay the first course of stones on top of the gravel. To determine how much stone you will need, see page 34. For taller walls, or those holding back soil on a steep slope, you will need to add a drainage pipe as shown on the previous page. Wear goggles or protective eyewear.

1. Lay the First Course. Dig the trench the width of the stone wall and about 6 inches deep. Lay the first course (or level of stones), choosing the largest stones for the outer edges. Fill in the middle area with the smaller stones.

2. Cut Stones to Fit. Shape stones by chipping off the edges with your brick hammer. To split larger stones, set them flat on the ground; score a line with a cold chisel and hammer; and then place the chisel in the center of the scored line and strike it firmly with the hammer.

3. Fill the Gaps between Stones. Chink large gaps in the wall with stone chips by hammering an appropriately sized chip into the space. When you reach the top layer of the wall, the stone chips are also useful to raise a stone slab to make it level with the string guide.

4. Complete the Top Course. For structural stability, choose and place stones so that the vertical joints alternate between courses, rather than run in a straight line. While you want to keep the middle courses fairly level, the top course, where the string is set, is most important.

Dry-Laid Stone Retaining Walls

Dry-laid stone walls are not mortared together. They look beautiful as retaining walls on a short slope or running across a hill to create terraces. However, since they are not strengthened by mortar, dry-laid stone retaining walls should not be more than about 3 feet tall. A 3-foot-tall dry-laid stone wall should be at least 2 feet thick at its base. While it does not require a concrete footing, a base of gravel will improve drainage and reduce frost heaving. Dig an 8-inch trench, and fill it with 4 inches of gravel as a base for the first course of stone. A wall of native stone will be in better harmony with its surroundings.

Building a dry-laid stone wall is similar to solving a jigsaw puzzle because you need to choose stones that fit together nicely. The bottom row of the wall should have the largest stones. The wall should consist of two vertical stacks, or wythes, with large bond stones that extend into the side of the slope placed every several feet. (These serve the same purpose as the deadmen discussed in "Building Wood Retaining Walls," page 22.) For extra wall stability, lay the stones so that they tip slightly into the slope at a rate of about 2 inches for every foot of wall height. If a sloping front bothers you, tilt the inside layer of the wall and build the outer layer so it stands vertically. In this instance, however, the footing must extend beyond the wall into the slope. As you build, backfill any space between the wall and the slope with gravel. As you work, add soil to pockets between the stones. If you want plants growing out of the wall, add them as you build. Top the wall with a row of flat capstones to cover the entire thickness of the wall. Some stonemasons like to set the capstones in mortar to prevent moisture from seeping into the wall and to keep the stones from being knocked off.

Plant dry-laid stone walls by filling voids with potting mix. Use heat and drought-tolerant plants.

Dry-Laid Stone Retaining Wall

A dry-laid stone retaining wall should lean slightly into the slope to give it stability. Use a large bond stone every few rows to help anchor the structure. The gravel backfill and perforated pipe help drain water away from the wall.

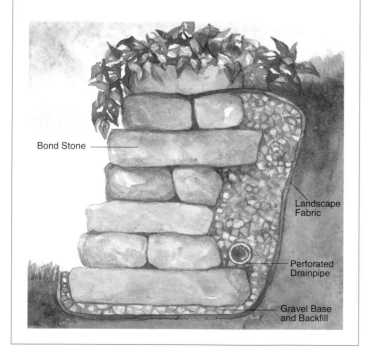

Bond Stone

Landscape Fabric

Perforated Drainpipe

Gravel Base and Backfill

This formal stone retaining wall is an attractive boundary for the patio. The wall blends beautifully with the flagstone paving, while the lush plantings of hosta, sweet woodruff, and other shade-loving plants soften the extensive stonework.

The fresh, white picket fence sets off this cottage garden profusion of orange and yellow lilies and daylilies, with red bee balm in the background, making a memorable garden vignette.

Designing Fences

Erecting a fence is the quickest and generally easiest way to define the boundary of your property. To be a successful part of a landscape design, a fence should be planned to complement the architecture of your house, possibly even echoing a distinctive design feature. Also bear in mind the character of your neighborhood and region. Your fence may be beautiful in and of itself but look out of place in the neighborhood where you live. In addition to style, other considerations for making a fence harmonious with its surroundings include height, color, and material.

Many Design Options Exist

With the considerations mentioned above in mind, the possibilities for fence designs are limitless. Traditional options include wrought iron, wooden pickets (or palings), stockade, split-rail, double- and triple-bar ranch fences, and even chain-link fences. Within those basic styles are infinite variations. For example, iron can be wrought in fanciful designs from modern clean-cut to the fancy curlicues of the Romanesque style. Picket points can take the form of arrows, fleurs-de-lis, or any other design. The pickets can be spaced in a variety of ways. Stockade fences can be closed- or open-board, or have angled paling boards. To add extra charm and interest, a solid wooden fence can be topped with lattice.

Function Dictates Style. The primary purpose of the fence will influence your design. For privacy you'll want a tall, solid fence. If the goal is to keep the dog contained, the fence can have open slats, but you'll have to think about whether the dog is likely to jump over a low fence or burrow underneath. Rabbits, woodchucks, and mice may also burrow under fences. To keep rabbits and woodchucks out, you'll need a wire mesh no larger than 1½ inches buried at least 6 inches under the soil. To exclude mice the mesh should be a fine ¼ inch, and the barrier should extend 1 foot below the soil. Deer can jump 8 feet straight into the air. To keep them out you need a very tall fence or a fence combined with other deterrents.

In addition to fencing the boundary of your property, you may want a fence to define a smaller space within your garden. In small gardens where there isn't room to plant a hedge behind a flower border, a fence creates an excellent backdrop for the flowers. You may be able to optimize your space by planting a border along both sides of the fence.

Installing a Fence

The redwood picket fence illustrated below is based on photographs from 1881 and a few existing old pickets. This low fence marks the property line and contains children or pets without obstructing the view of the lovely Victorian house. To calculate the amount of materials, determine what it will take to build one fence bay (usually 8 feet from post to post). Then multiply that figure by the number of bays needed to complete the fence.

1. Install the Posts. Mark the course of the fence using stakes and string, and then mark the location for each post (usually 6 to 8 feet apart). Dig postholes three times the width of the posts and 1 foot below the frost line. Set the posts; check that they are plumb; and pour the concrete.

2. Build the Frame. Measure and cut the top and bottom rails. Fasten the top rail in place, then the bottom rail. Top rails are butt-joined over the posts and mitered at the corners. Bottom rails can be toenailed, fastened using a block or metal brace, or inset into the post by cutting a dado or notch.

3. Nail in the Pickets. Tack a string across several bays to mark the bottom fence line. Starting at the end, begin nailing up the fence palings. Every few feet, check the level of the vertical edge of the last board you've fastened, and adjust as needed. Mark the bottom edge of the fence to match the contour of the land. Trim as needed.

4. Finish the Fence. Fasten the remaining pickets, and then build and hang a gate. Install any necessary gate hardware. Remove any stakes or strings used as guides. This picket fence perfectly complements the style of the house and enhances the landscape. (A furniture company custom-cut these pickets.)

Fence Anatomy

The main components of a board fence are pickets, horizontal rails, a top rail to protect the end grain of the pickets from moisture, the kickboard, and the support post.

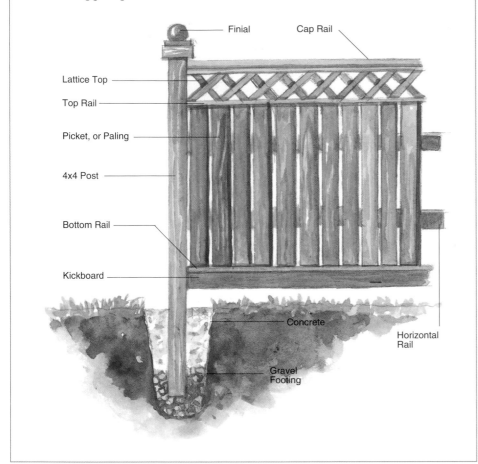

- Finial
- Cap Rail
- Lattice Top
- Top Rail
- Picket, or Paling
- 4x4 Post
- Bottom Rail
- Kickboard
- Concrete
- Gravel Footing
- Horizontal Rail

Include a Beginning and End. A fence should have a logical starting and ending point. A common mistake is to erect a fence to block an unwanted view without connecting it to any other feature in the garden. This approach tends to look jarring. Far better is to connect the fence at both ends to an architectural feature or to have the fence run full circle and connect to itself.

Like a chain, a fence is only as strong as its weakest component. If you are building a fence, be sure to choose strong posts and sink them properly into the ground. Erect fence posts the same way you would install posts to support a wooden retaining wall, as described on page 22. If you're building a wooden fence, you will save money if you design the fence so you can use standard lengths of lumber. Otherwise you'll waste too much time measuring and cutting, and you'll end up with a lot of wasted wood.

Before you begin a do-it-yourself fencing project, check with local authorities for relevant codes and ordinances. Height and placement regulations (especially required setbacks from property lines) vary from community to community, and some residential neighborhoods have their own covenants.

Building Fences on Slopes

A slope presents a special challenge for fence design as fence sections are generally straight and parallel with the ground. Three possible solutions include stepping the fence down the slope, allowing gaps to occur as the slope progresses downward; building the fence to follow the hillside so that the top of the fence is angled at the same degree as the slope; and custom-building the fence so each paling touches the ground, creating a wavy line across the fence top and bottom.

Stepped Fencing

Sloped Fencing

Contour Fencing

Designing Gates

The garden gate meets many needs, from practical to aesthetic to psychological. It is a place of romance—where else would an ardent suitor steal a kiss or wait for a late-night romantic tryst but by the garden gate?

On the purely practical side, a gate allows passage to and between a front and back garden. This functional aspect is closely tied to a gate's symbolic meaning. A locked, solid gate set in a high wall or fence provides a sense of privacy, enclosure, and security. A gate with an open design, even when set into a solid wall, has a welcoming air about it.

Gates Conceal Secret Gardens or Welcome Visitors

An open gate beckons; a tall, solid gate adds mystery, suggesting the entrance to a secret garden. It can guide the eye to a focal point, or add charm, intimacy, drama, or panache.

Gates, even short ones that stand only 3 feet high, serve as important transition points from the garden to the outside world or from one part of the garden to another. They define boundaries while linking the two areas together. For that reason, gates and pathways tend to go together in a landscape design.

Don't confine your gates to the perimeter of your property. Use them within your garden as well, to divide space visually and to mark the boundaries between different areas or garden rooms.

Consider Function and Aesthetics.

Gates can be adapted to many different settings. If you have a patio that leads to a lawn, for example, consider planting a low evergreen hedge to frame the edges of the patio, with a gate in the opening that leads to the lawn. The gated hedge performs two functions. First, it breaks up the horizontal monotony created by the patio spreading into the lawn. Second, it creates activity areas by setting the patio apart as a special place for sitting and dining, with the gate providing access to the rest of the garden.

Make sure your gate is wide enough to wheel your garden wagon through. If it is the main access to your property, you may want it to be wide enough for two people to pass. Narrow gates, however, are appropriate for interior passages.

This decorative gate, embellished with a profusion of climbing roses, is a welcoming beginning to the garden experience. It suggests a garden inside that is designed and planted with style.

A lattice fence and gate provide privacy and security, at the same time allowing tantalizing glimpses into the garden. The pretty fretwork pattern is an added bonus.

Gates are hung from posts, which are generally made of metal, brick, wood, or concrete. The diameter of the posts should be determined by the width of the gate. A gate 3 feet wide or smaller should be mounted on a 4x4 post sunk 1½ feet into the ground for stability. Gates 3 to 4 feet wide need the extra strength of a 6x6 post sunk 2 feet deep. There should be a 3-inch gap between the bottom of the gate and the ground to allow for easy opening and closing.

Allow the concrete to set completely before you hang the gate. Thoroughly read the instructions on the bag of concrete to know how much time is required.

Once the gate is hung and you've made any necessary adjustments so that it swings properly, install the latch. Use galvanized screws that are as long as possible without protruding from the opposite side.

To prevent the gate from swinging past its closed position and putting unnecessary strain on the hinges, attach a vertical strip of wood to the gate post to stop the gate when it closes.

1. Space the Posts. Lay the gate on the ground, and position the posts on each side, allowing enough space for the hinges and latch. Make sure the tops and bottoms of the posts are even. Nail temporary battens onto the posts as shown. (The bottom batten should be at the bottom of the gate.)

2. Dig postholes, and then set the posts on a bed of gravel, making sure the bottom batten is 3 inches off the ground and that the posts are plumb and level. Secure the posts with braces and stakes as temporary supports, and then fill the holes with concrete. Check again for plumb and level before the concrete sets.

3. Hang the Gate. When the concrete has completely cured, remove the braces and battens, attach the hinges (with the gate attached) to the post, and then attach the latch. The job is easier if one person holds the gate in position while the other drills the screw holes and attaches the hardware.

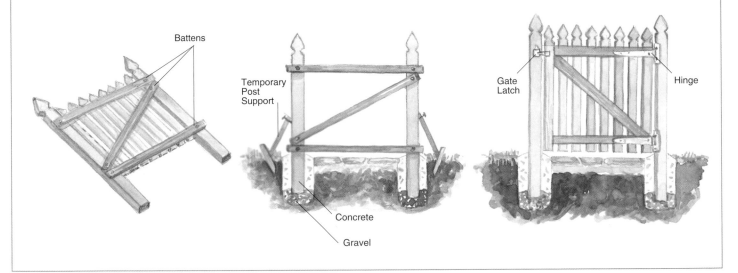

Battens

Temporary Post Support

Concrete

Gravel

Gate Latch

Hinge

A Style of Gate for Every Landscape

Gates come in an endless variety of styles and sizes. Massive wrought-iron gates mark the entrances to many large Victorian parks and private estates. Painted, slatted gates set in white picket fences tend to belong with small, intimate cottages or traditional country homes. The gate to a vegetable plot might be rough-hewn, in keeping with an untreated wooden fence designed to keep out wildlife. Japanese moon gates have cutout circles symbolic of the full moon. These circles may be open or filled in with a fretted design of wood or iron to add visual interest and increase security.

Choose your gates to fit the style of your garden, but don't be afraid to have fun. For example, use a terra-cotta color to blend with a Spanish-style house, or set a light-colored gate against a dark backdrop of heavy foliage.

Manufactured or Custom-Made Gates. Good fencing companies usually offer a great range of gate styles and materials. Old wrought-iron gates are popular items in antique shops.

Whatever you decide for your garden gates, let them be more than functional. Allow the gates to convey the subliminal message you want for your garden, thus enhancing your environment.

Designing Trellises

Trellises were a key element in Renaissance gardens and continued in popularity through the eighteenth century. Trellises enjoyed a resurgence of popularity in the late-nineteenth century, but never to the extent of earlier times.

Trellises can lend an air of magic and mystery to a garden. Generally we think of trellises in terms of the prefabricated sheets of diamond- or square-grid lattice and the fan-shaped supports for training climbers, both of which are readily available at home and garden centers in both wood and plastic. Lacking a pattern book, most gardeners are unaware of the incredible variety of designs, patterns, and optical illusions that can be created with trellises.

This pergola, with its pointed, gothic arch has a ceremonial air. The climbing roses turn the passage from one part of the garden to another into a celebration.

Use Trellises to Divide Space or Provide Privacy

A trellis screen is a wonderfully airy way to achieve privacy or to partition off a space. The lath slats of lattice interrupt the view without totally obscuring it, creating the effect of a transparent curtain. Left bare, the pretty design of diamonds or squares makes an attractive effect. Covered in vines or decorated with hanging baskets, a trellis screen is enchanting.

Cover a Wall with a Trellis. The art of treillage, as the French call it, is not limited to screens. Cover a wall or fence with a trellis. Arrange the trellis pieces to create an optical illusion of an archway. Paint a realistic mural of the make-believe garden space beyond. Or use a trellis for the walls of a gazebo to provide support for climbing plants.

Typical Trellis Design

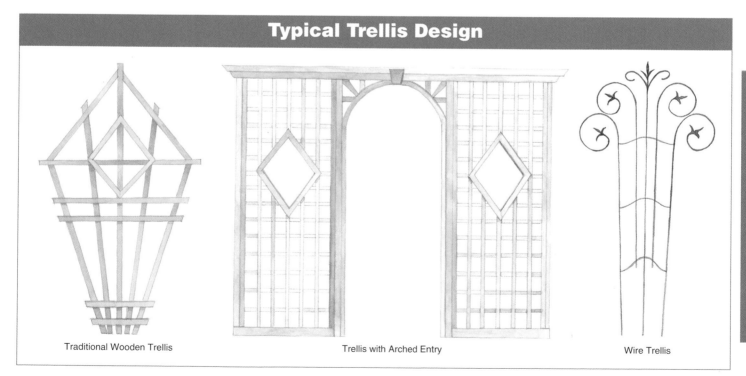

Traditional Wooden Trellis   Trellis with Arched Entry   Wire Trellis

chapter 4
trees & shrubs

These formal hedges serve two purposes: in surrounding trees, they serve as living borders that call attention to the trees themselves; the placement of the hedges helps to guide visitors through the garden.

Pruning Structure

Like a fine face, a beautiful garden must have good bone structure. The "bones" are the year-round features: paths, steps, hedges, walls, fences, and other permanent elements that provide structure and a sense of unity. The other major components of a garden's bones are trees and shrubs.

In old, established gardens, you may need to remove or rejuvenate overgrown trees and shrubs to reclaim the original structure of the garden. If you are starting from scratch, you should plan the trees and shrubs that will define the structure of the landscape before you begin thinking of details such as ground covers, perennials, and annuals. Choose trees and shrubs that will help define spaces, provide focal points, or serve as a background foil to other plantings.

Highlight Plants with Unusual Shapes

Don't overlook the importance of key plants with a bold or unusual shape. A tree or shrub that naturally grows in a striking form, such as the pagoda dogwood (*Cornus alternifolia*), or a spectacular specimen tree, such as a monumental chestnut or beech tree, makes a fascinating focal point, giving structure and visual direction to the overall design. If your property already has a significant, established tree, try to design your landscape to emphasize that asset. A pragmatic thinker may believe it's a waste of time and money to plant a tree that won't come into its full beauty until he or she is long gone. While understandable, that attitude is unfortunate because American gardens are not being planted with the spectacular but slow-growing trees that take years to mature.

Choosing Trees and Shrubs

Trees and shrubs have the potential to be the greatest asset in your garden, or the greatest liability if you do not choose the right ones. Spend the time to determine which plants will do well in your climate, including the specific soil, water, and light conditions on your property. Most climate zone maps indicate a plant's tolerance to cold. The American Horticultural Society recently introduced a map and rating system that records heat tolerance as well. (See page 95 for the American Horticultural Society Plant Heat-Zone Map.) If you live in a region with hot, humid summers, make sure the trees you select are able to endure the extreme heat and humidity.

Determine the Plant's Purpose

If you want to plant a tree or shrub as a focal point in the center of a lawn, you can choose a large spreading specimen that will become ever more spectacular as it grows. But if you want to plant a tree along a driveway or patio, don't choose one with invasive roots. For example, weeping willow roots search insistently for water, even boring through pipes, and can heave up a concrete walkway or crack a house foundation. For a patio tree, you want one that will provide shade as well as visual interest such as pretty flowers, fruit, foliage, and/or bark. Stay away from messy trees that shed regularly or drop sticky fruit or sap, creating the need for frequent cleanup on paved surfaces.

Winter is the best season to evaluate your landscape. In spring and summer, lush foliage and lavish floral displays can disguise many design problems. But once the foliage falls and the flowers fade, the true structure of the garden is clearly visible.

Evergreen trees are an obvious choice for maintaining color and interest in the fall and winter garden. The Colorado blue spruce (*Picea pungens* 'Glauca') is a wonderful choice both for its almost-perfect Christmas tree form and its silvery blue color. The golden yellow foliage of *Chamaecyparis lawsoniana* 'Lutea', brings a sense of sunshine into even the drabbest winter day. Evergreen hedges are real assets in the winter garden.

Deciduous Trees with Strong Silhouettes. Good possibilities include Japanese maple (*Acer palmatum*), with its marvelous twisting branches, and Harry Lauder's walking stick (*Corylus avellana* 'Contorta'). Another twisted wonder is the willow *Salix matsudana* 'Tortuosa'.

Berry-Bearing Plants. Berry-bearing shrubs and trees are a delight in a winter landscape. Hollies, *Nandina*, *Cotoneaster*, and *Pyracantha* all hold their berries into winter. Also look for *Viburnum dilatatum* 'Erie'. In addition to their visual appeal, berry-laden trees and shrubs attract birds.

Colorful Bark. Many deciduous trees and shrubs have colorful bark that stands out dramatically in a winter landscape. One excellent choice for beautiful bark is the red twig dogwood (*Cornus alba*), a small, multi-stemmed shrub with striking red twigs. Another interesting dogwood member is the golden-twig dogwood (*Cornus stolonifera* 'Flaviramea'), which has bright yellow winter shoots.

Birch trees are lovely in the winter landscape. There is a choice of bark colors from dark gray to silvery gold to the classic white. Some varieties of crape myrtle (*Lagerstroemia indica*) have beautiful bark streaked with green, gold, and pink. Moosewood or striped maple (*Acer pensylvanicum*) has green- and white-striped bark; *A. pensylvanicum* 'Erythrocladum' has coral red bark striped with silvery white.

Peeling Bark. Trees with peeling bark are another interesting phenomenon. Look for the paperbark maple (*A. griseum*), which peels off thin flakes of orange brown bark, and Heritage river birch (*Betula nigra* 'Heritage'), which exfoliates at an early age and peels off beautiful flakes of salmon-white and orange-brown bark.

Above *Chamaecyparis* 'Aurea nana' (Japanese false cypress), center

Left Bark of *Betula papyrifera* (birch)

Below *Nandina* (heavenly bamboo)

Create a View or a Border, or Both. Plant an avenue of trees to create a vista in your garden. Line your driveway with flowering trees such as crab apples for a spectacular "welcome home" in spring when the blossoms are open and a cool, shady drive in the summer. Add interest to an expanse of lawn with a grove of trees. Place a bench among the trees, and you'll have a special shaded seat.

Trees and shrubs are excellent for providing mass in your landscape. Include shrubs and even small trees in flower borders to provide interest in winter and to anchor the design. Border a bed with a low-growing shrub such as dwarf boxwood or *Santolina* to frame and give definition to the plantings. Line a path with scented shrubs such as lavender or plant a bulky shrub at the curve of a winding path to obscure the view around a corner.

Obscure Eyesores and Save Energy. Trees can be useful to screen an unattractive view, lower noise levels, cut the wind, and provide shade. A deciduous tree planted near the house, especially on the south side, can save heating and cooling costs. Likewise, a row of trees planted in the path of prevailing winds can deflect the icy gusts, thus helping to cut down on heating costs.

Design for the Seasons

Plant trees and shrubs for seasonal interest such as spectacular autumn color, spring or summer flowers, or a compelling silhouette in winter. Choose a shrub for its fragrant flowers or foliage. Place a sweet-smelling shrub under a window, or beside a patio or outdoor seating area so you can enjoy the scent. Some trees, such as the crab apple or dogwood, shine in more than one season.

Viburnum is another delightful plant that gives good value for the space it uses. This is a large plant family with species such as *V. lentago* that is hardy down to Zone 2, to more tender specimens that need Zone 8 or warmer. Among the excellent choices for the home garden is the doublefile viburnun (*V. plicatum f. tomentosum*). In spring it is covered in white, lacecap-like flowers. The crinkled leaves (the Latin name *plicatum* refers to the leaf's pleated look) are a joy throughout the summer, and then in autumn, bright red fruit lights up the shrub.

For tight spaces, consider *Viburnum dilatatum* 'Catskill', a compact shrub that takes at least 15 years to reach a height of 5 feet with an 8-foot spread. The dark green foliage takes on shades of red and yellow in fall. Abundant dark red fruit persists until midwinter. *Viburnum* 'Conoy' grows about as big as 'Catskill.' Its glossy, evergreen foliage is the perfect backdrop to the creamy white flowers in the spring and the brilliant red berries in autumn.

The bright orange Japanese maple tree in the distance is the focal point of this path. Notice how the yellow flowering tree frames the path and points the way to the exclamation point in the distance.

The trees in this landscape screen the view of the house beyond. Although the shrubs in front of the tree stand are not fully grown, they will grow into a continuous line and provide an understory for the larger trees.

Distinctive Trees

Too often a young tree or shrub is planted close to a building or fence with no allowance made for its growth over time. The ultimate size of a tree depends on many variables, including the quality of the soil, average temperatures, and the potential of each individual specimen. Some of the plants listed here may technically be shrubs, but because of their mature height, they are listed as trees.

Small Trees
(up to 30 feet tall)

- *Acer japonicum* (Japanese maple) Zones 6–9
- *A. tataricum ssp. ginnala*
  (Amur maple) Zones 3–7
- *Amelanchier laevis*
  (Allegheny serviceberry), Zones 4–9
- *Arbutus unedo* (strawberry tree) Zones 7–9
- *Cercis canadensis*
  (eastern redbud) Zones 4–9
- *Chionanthus retusus*
  (Chinese fringe tree) Zones 6–8
- *Cornus florida* (flowering dogwood) Zones 5–9
- *Franklinia alatamaha*
  (Franklin tree) Zones 5–8 or 9
- *Magnolia x soulangiana*
  (saucer magnolia) Zones 5–9
- *Magnolia stellata* (star magnolia) Zones 4–8
- *Malus sp.* (flowering crab apple) zones vary
  with species
- *Oxydendrum arboreum*
  (sourwood) Zones 5–9
- *Prunus x blireana*
  (flowering plum) Zones 5–8
- *Styrax japonicum*
  (Japanese snowbell) Zones 5–9

Medium to Large Trees
(30 feet and taller)

- *Acer rubrum* (red maple) Zones 3–9
- *Acer saccharinum* (silver maple) Zones 3–9
- *Albizia julibrissin*
  (silk tree or mimosa) Zones 6–10
- *Cercidiphyllum japonicum*
  (Katsura tree) Zones 4–8
- *Fraxinus pennsylvanica*
  (green ash) Zones 3–9
- *Ginkgo biloba*
  (ginkgo, maidenhair tree) Zones 4–9
- *Gleditsia triacanthos* (honey locust) Zones 4–9
- *Gymnocladus dioica*
  (Kentucky coffee tree) Zones 4–9
- *Halesia tetraptera*
  (Carolina silver bell) Zones 5–9
- *Koelreuteria paniculata*
  (varnish tree) Zones 5–9
- *Lagerstroemia indica* (crape myrtle) Zones 7–9
- *Nyssa sylvatica* (sour gum) Zones 4–9
- *Parrotia persica* (Persian ironwood) Zones 5–8
- *Sophora japonica* (pagoda tree) Zones 4–9
- Stewartia pseudocamellia Zones 5–8
- *Tilia cordata* (littleleaf linden) Zones 4–7
- *Zelkova serrata* (Japanese zelkova) Zones 5–9

Malus sylvestris (flowering crab apple)

Acer japonicum (Japanese maple)

Lagerstroemia indica (crape myrtle) with Spanish moss

Distinctive Shrubs

Shrubs with Attractive Flowers

- *Camellia japonica*, and *C. sasanqua* — Zones 7–10
- *Chaenomeles* (flowering quince) — Zones 5–9
- *Cytisus x praecox* (Warminster broom) — Zones 7–9
- *Daphne cneorum* (garland flower) — Zones 4–9
- *Deutzia gracilis* — Zones 4–9
- *Hamamelis x intermedia* (witch hazel) — Zones 5–9
- *Hydrangea macrophylla* — Zones 6–10
- *Hypericum sp.* (St.-John's-wort) — zones vary with species
- *Kalmia latifolia* (mountain laurel) — Zones 4–9
- *Kerria japonica* (Japanese rose or kerria) — Zones 4–9
- *Lagerstroemia indica* (crape myrtle) — Zones 7–9
- *Philadelphus* species and cultivars (sweet mock orange) — Zones 4–8
- *Pieris japonica* (Japanese andromeda) — Zones 6–8
- *Potentilla fruticosa* (shrubby cinquefoil) — Zones 2–7
- *Prunus triloba* (flowering almond) — Zones 3–8
- *Spiraea japonica* (Japanese spirea) — Zones 4–8
- *Viburnum* species (viburnum), — zones vary with species
- *Weigela florida* (weigela) — Zones 5–9

Shrubs with Attractive Berries

- *Berberis darwinii* — Zones 8–10
- *Berberis wilsoniae* (Wilson barberry) — Zones 7–10
- *Callicarpa americana* (beautyberry) — Zones 7–10
- *Callicarpa bodinieri* (beautyberry) — Zones 6–8, good to Zone 10 in West
- *Cotoneaster lucidus* (hedge cotoneaster) — Zones 4–7
- *Cotoneaster salicifolius* (willowleaf cotoneaster) — Zones 6–8 in the East; 6–10 in the West.
- *Euonymus alata* (burning bush) — Zones 4–9
- *Ilex species* (holly) — zones vary with species
- *Mahonia aquifolium* (Oregon grape) — Zones 5–9
- *Mahonia bealei* — Zones 7–9
- *Nandina domestica* (heavenly bamboo) — Zones 7–10
- *Photinia serratifolia* (Chinese photinia) — Zones 7–9 in the East; 7–10 in the West
- *Pyracantha coccinea* (scarlet firethorn) — Zones 6–9
- *Rhus typhina* (staghorn sumac) — Zones 4–8
- *Viburnum* species (viburnum) — zones vary with species

Chaenomeles (flowering quince)

Pyracantha (firethorn) in winter

Adding Hedges

Hedges are invaluable in the landscape to screen unwanted views or high winds, to define garden spaces, to frame vistas, and to serve as a backdrop to borders or decorative elements such as sculpture. Traditionally we think of a hedge as a neatly pruned row of one species of plant. While that approach creates a tidy, uniform look that is ideal for formal settings, there is no rule against combining different shrubs with a variety of leaf colors and textures to create a hedge with a tapestry effect. You can either shear the plants for a tailored look or allow the shrubs to billow in their natural form for a soft, informal backdrop.

Plants That Live Longer

The natural inclination when choosing a tree or shrub for a hedge is to choose a plant that will grow as fast as possible. While the quick results are gratifying, the downside is that faster-growing plants tend to be shorter-lived. Slow-growing yew and boxwood, which can survive for hundreds of years, are the traditional shrubs used for hedges because they live so long. For this reason, boxwoods need only occasional pruning to keep them within bounds. As you consider all the wonderful plants available for creating hedges, weigh the pros and cons of the faster-growing hedging plants versus slower-growing plants with greater longevity.

This low-maintenance hedge, top, is also long-lived, thanks to the classic combination of slow-growing boxwood (*Buxus*) interplanted with columnar yew (*Taxus*).

A "wild" hedge of mixed plantings, left, is a garden in itself. Some of the shrubs shown here include roses, forsythia, andromeda, and peony.

Hedgerows: Underused

Another option for a living wall that is too seldom exercised in American gardens is a hedgerow. These are the mixed plantings of trees and shrubs that line the country roads and divide the fields in rural England and parts of Europe. In addition to being a fascinating combination of plants, hedgerows are wonderful habitats for a variety of birds, small animals, and other wildlife; they provide food, shelter, and protected travel routes.

There are two approaches to planting a hedgerow. The first is to select the trees, shrubs, and vines you want and plant them in a random mixture. Space them half the distance recommended by the supplier. Once the plants have reached the height and width you want, shear them periodically to maintain the shape. Don't be shy about cutting back the trees. They will adapt and grow appropriately for a hedge.

Planting a Hedge or Hedgerow

Planting a hedge or hedgerow takes a little more care than simply putting in one or two plants at random because you want the plants to follow the line of the hedge and to be spaced properly.

To work out the number of plants you need, first find out the expected mature width of the shrub. In theory you should then simply divide the length of the hedge by the projected width of each plant to find out how many plants to buy. However, you can't count on a plant ever growing to its optimal size. If soil, light, or moisture conditions are not ideal, the shrub may take years to fulfill its potential—or it may never reach it. Because you definitely want the plants to touch and even overlap to make an unbroken hedge, reduce the average expected width of each plant by about one third, and then do the division. For example, Japanese holly (*Ilex crenata*) is listed as having a spread of 10 feet at maturity. Figure

Hedges Made of Conifers

With regular pruning, some of these plants can be kept the size of medium to large shrubs.

■ *Cephalotaxus fortunei* (Chinese plum yew) slow growing	Zones 7–9
■ *Chamaecyparis lawsoniana* (Lawson false cypress or Port Orford cedar) medium growth rate	Zones 5–9
■ *C. x Cupressocyparis leylandii* (Leyland cypress) very fast growing	Zones 6–10
■ *Cupressus macrocarpa* (Monterey cypress) growth rate varies with cultivars	Zones 7–9
■ *Juniperus chinensis* (Chinese juniper) slow to medium growth rate	Zones 4–10
■ *Juniperus scopulorum* (Rocky Mountain juniper) slow-growing	Zones 4–10
■ *Podocarpus macrophylla* (southern yew) slow growing	Zones 7–10
■ *Pseudotsuga menziesii* (Douglas fir) medium growth rate	Zones 4–7
■ *Taxus baccata* (English yew) slow growing	Zones 5–8 in the East; 5–10 in the West
■ *Thuja plicata* (western red cedar) growth varies with cultivars	Zones 6–7
■ *Tsuga canadensis* (Canada hemlock) medium growth rate	Zones 4–7

Podocarpus macrophyllus (Southern yew), above.

Chamaecyparis (false cedar), center right.

on planting a maximum of 7 feet apart—and closer if you want a fully closed-in hedge more quickly. Divide the length of the hedge by 7 to get the number of plants needed. If your holly hedge will be 100 feet long, then you would need 14 or 15 plants. Because holly is such a slow growing plant, you might want to add another 3 to 5 plants to shorten the gaps. In that case, plant 20 hollies 5 feet apart. Commercial landscapers typically plant shrubs much closer together than necessary to get a filled-in hedge more quickly.

As a homeowner, you probably want to compromise between using a minimum number of plants and jamming them in tightly for an instant effect.

Leave Planting to the Birds: Plow and Perch. The second technique of planting a hedgerow is rather fun because it leaves a lot to chance and nature. Called the plow-and-perch method, you create conditions that encourage the birds to "plant" the hedgerow for you. In summer or early autumn, till the line where you want your hedgerow to grow, making the soil receptive to seeds. Rent or borrow a large, heavy-duty rototiller that can cut through sod with ease. Mount posts at 15 foot intervals along the line, and attach a double row of strong string or wire between the posts. Seed- and fruit-eating birds will perch along the line, distributing plant seeds with their droppings. There are several advantages to the plow-perch method of planting a hedgerow:

- Less work. It requires less trouble and less expense than seeking out and purchasing plants suitable for a hedgerow.

- Birds will do the job. The seeds sown are of plants definitely favored by local birds.

- Plants will thrive in local conditions. The plants are native, and so are well suited to the area where they will be growing.

- Transplant shock eliminated. These seed-grown species should mature as quickly as those planted from rootstocks because they won't undergo transplant shock.

A windscreen of mature lilacs separate a field from the road. When allowed to grow without pruning, these shrubs eventually reach the height of small trees.

Before you purchase a woody plant, take the time to closely examine the condition of its root system or rootball. Container and balled-and-burlapped plants should show evidence of regular watering. Bare-root plants should be kept damp. If you are considering a container-grown plant, slide the plant out of its pot. Look for symmetrical roots that are white and plump, not dried out. Cut away the twine, basket wire, and burlap on balled-and-burlapped plants after placing the plant in the hole.

Container

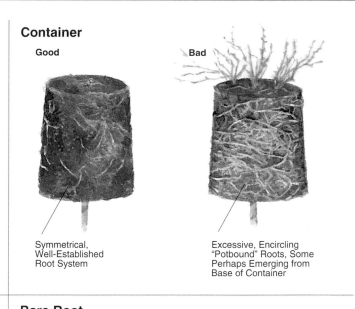

Good

Bad

Symmetrical, Well-Established Root System

Excessive, Encircling "Potbound" Roots, Some Perhaps Emerging from Base of Container

Balled and Burlapped

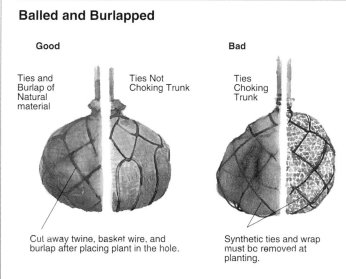

Good

Bad

Ties and Burlap of Natural material

Ties Not Choking Trunk

Ties Choking Trunk

Cut away twine, basket wire, and burlap after placing plant in the hole.

Synthetic ties and wrap must be removed at planting.

Bare Root

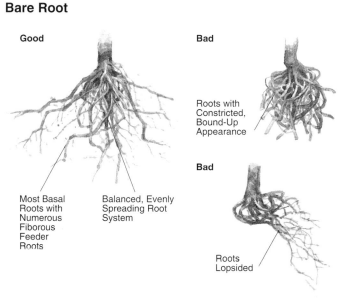

Good

Bad

Most Basal Roots with Numerous Fiborous Feeder Roots

Balanced, Evenly Spreading Root System

Roots with Constricted, Bound-Up Appearance

Bad

Roots Lopsided

Purchasing Tips

Once you've decided on the trees or shrubs that will best suit your purpose in the garden, it's time to make the purchase. Contrary to what instinct may tell you, the largest plant is not necessarily the best. The larger the specimen, the more transplant shock it will experience. In the case of big trees and shrubs, it can take two or three years from the time of planting before the plant will begin to grow vigorously. A small tree or shrub will usually adapt in one season. The result is that in just a few years, a smaller, less expensive tree will catch up in size to a larger one. Save money by purchasing small plants, and give yourself the pleasure of watching your garden grow.

Unless you want to nurse a sick plant back to health, pass by any plant that isn't thriving. Trees and shrubs are major investments, so it is worth paying a little extra to get top-quality plants. Shop only from the most reputable nurseries and mail-order catalogs, and check for a guarantee.

Avoid Trees with Injured Bark.
Inspect the bark of trees for signs of injury or mistreatment. A strong tree should be able to stand on its own without staking. If you see sunburn damage —indicated by split, flattened, or unusually dull-colored bark—find a different tree. Also look for signs of pests and diseases to avoid getting a weakened plant and introducing a problem into your own garden.

Planting a Hedge

First mark out the line where you want the hedge. If you are making a curved hedge, use a hose to mark out the line you want, and leave it in place until you are ready to dig. Once you have your plants, position them along the line, making the spaces between each as even as possible. Remember to allow growing space for the plants at each end; set these half the spacing distance in from the desired end of your hedge. Follow the appropriate directions for bare-root, balled-and-burlapped, or container-grown plants. (See pages 55–57.) Mulch along the row with an organic material such as straw, shredded bark, or shredded leaves. The mulch should be 4 to 6 inches deep to be the most effective in minimizing evaporation and smothering weeds.

1. Mark the Hedge Line. Run string between stakes along the hedge line. Either dig a trench beneath the string or position the plants precisely using a tape measure. Dig a hole for each plant, putting the soil on a tarp.

2. Plant Each Shrub. Break up the root ball with your fingers. Position the plant straight in the hole, and backfill until the crown of the plant is at the same depth as it was growing in the pot.

3. Water and Mulch. Water each plant thoroughly as you dig it in. Allow the water to disperse in the hole, and water again. Apply an organic mulch around each plant and between plants along the row.

4. Finish the Planting. Check again that the plants are in a straight line. Dig new holes if necessary, and replant any shrubs that are out of line. Pull up the stakes and string, and fold up the tarp.

Planting Basics

The rules for planting trees and shrubs have changed. Today, instead of recommending a planting hole twice the width and depth of the rootball, experts suggest digging a hole just big enough to hold the plant. That way the soil won't settle.

Evidence suggests that trees and shrubs grow better if they are planted directly into the native soil rather than into amended soil. Ultimately you want the tree's roots to extend well beyond the original hole. If the soil in the hole is much richer than the surrounding native soil, the roots will avoid growing beyond that luxurious environment. The result is that they become rootbound in their own hole. These facts make it all the more important to choose trees and shrubs that are suited to the native soil. You'll experience nothing but frustration if you select a tree or shrub that prefers sandy soil and plant it in clay, or plant a shrub that needs acidic soil (a low pH) in alkaline soil. If your soil is heavy, plant trees and shrubs about 2 inches above the level it grew in the nursery field. Look for the soil-line stain on the trunk for a guide.

Don't Prune at Planting Time
The conventional wisdom used to dictate pruning back trees at planting time to create a balance between roots and foliage. More recent evidence shows that the extra foliage produces hormones that encourage root regeneration. If there are any branches that are broken, remove them; leave the rest alone.

How to Plant Bare-Root Stock

Before you purchase a woody plant, take the time to closely examine the condition of its root system or rootball. Container and balled-and-burlapped plants should show evidence of regular watering. Bare-root plants should be kept damp. If you are considering a container-grown plant, slide the plant out of its pot. Look for symmetrical roots that are white and plump, not dried out. Cut away the twine, basket wire, and burlap on balled-and-burlapped plants after placing the plant in the hole.

Step 1: Check the Depth

Place the roots on a cone of undisturbed soil. Lay a shovel across the hole, and make sure the crown is at or slightly above ground level.

Root Flare at or Slightly Above Ground Level

Step2: Fill the Hole

After removing any broken roots, use your hands to pack soil in and around the roots, firming the soil as you go to eliminate air pockets.

Step 3: Finish Planting

When the hole is half full of soil, water well. After the water seeps down, add the remaining soil and create a moat. Tamp the soil down with your foot. Apply several inches of mulch around the tree or shrub, keeping it about 2 inches from the trunk.

How to Plant a Balled-and-Burlapped Stock

Trees that are grown at the nursery are often balled and burlapped after they are dug from the ground. This means that the roots are enclosed in a ball of original soil and the ball is wrapped in burlap and tied together.

Like any newly planted tree or shrub, balled-and-burlapped plants need extra care their first year or so. Be especially careful with watering. Many balled-and-burlapped plants are field-grown in heavy clay soil, which absorbs water slowly. If your native soil is lighter, it will take in water much more quickly. When you water, make sure the rootball is getting properly saturated. If in doubt about whether you have watered enough, gently insert a dry wooden stick, such as a paint stirrer, into the soil. Pull it out after an hour or so. If the soil is moist enough, the stick will have absorbed the moisture and will have become slightly darker.

1. Dig the Hole. Remove enough soil to make a hole that is about the same depth as the rootball and twice as wide. Put the soil on the tarp. The bottom of the hole should be covered with firm, undisturbed soil.

2. Check the Hole. Hold the plant at the base of the trunk, and place it in the hole to check the depth, making sure the crown is slightly above ground level. Add water until it pools in the bottom of the hole.

3. Remove the Burlap. Untie the wrapping, or cut the cage off, and remove the burlap from the plant. Fill the hole with soil from the tarp, and tamp it down with your foot to eliminate air holes and stabilize the plant.

4. Water and Mulch. Build a shallow moat around the trunk. Fill the moat with water, and let it dissipate. Put several inches of mulch around the trunk, but do not pack the mulch right up against the trunk.

How to Plant Container-Grown Stock

To get the plant off to a good start, loosen up its roots when you take it out of the container. Untangle any roots that are growing in circles around the bottom of the pot. Dig the planting hole to accommodate the roots stretched out to their full length. (You can dig special trenches to accommodate one or two extra-long roots.) Place the soil from the hole on a tarp. Don't be shy about pruning, tearing, and cutting the roots. This seemingly rough handling will stimulate the plant to grow important new feeder roots.

1. Remove the Plant. Water the plant; then lay the pot on its side and slide the plant out. If the plant doesn't come out easily, tap the sides of the container or cut open the pot.

2. Break Up the Rootball. Make several vertical cuts deep into the soil mass, and firmly tease the roots outward by hand. Thick, heavily tangled roots require more and deeper cuts.

3. Check the Depth. Lay a shovel across the hole. With the roots resting on undisturbed soil, the crown should be slightly above ground level. If necessary, build up the soil under the root mass.

4. Plant the Shrub. Without disturbing the plant, return half of the soil on the tarp to the hole, and gently tamp it down with your foot to stabilize the plant and eliminate air holes in the soil.

5. Water. Pour enough water into the half-filled hole so that it pools. Wait for the water to dissipate; then fill the hole with the remainder of the soil.

6. Create a Moat. Using the shovel, build a shallow, moat-like depression around the trunk. Add more water, and let that settle. Note that the trunk's crown remains above ground level.

Plan to make the stakes as short as possible. Otherwise, when it sways in the wind, the tree trunk may be damaged by rubbing against the edges of the top of the stakes. If you are just anchoring the roots in place, 36-inch stakes will suffice. Drive stakes into the ground about 18 inches deep. To find the proper height for stakes used to support tall, weak trunks, hold the trunk in one hand, pull the canopy gently so that the trunk is bent, and then release it. The point where the trunk returns to upright when the top is released is where it should be

tied. Always use at least two stakes per tree. Be sure to position the stakes just outside the rootball; you won't damage the roots, and the firm soil will give better support.

Note: Supports should be loose to allow flexing in the wind

3" Layer of Mulch at Least 2" from Trunk

Root Flare at Ground Level or Slightly Above

Fabric Looped Loosely Around Trunk

Rubber or Vinyl Hose

Firm, Undisturbed Cone of Original Soil

3" Layer of Mulch at Least 2" from Trunk

Root Flare at Ground Level or Slightly Above

Firm, Undisturbed Original Soil

Bare-Root Tree
(or tree with a small root system or with a loose rootball)

Top-Heavy Tree
(stakes allowing wind flexing driven in outside the root system)

Bare-Root Tree
(or tree with a small root system or with a loose rootball or tree planted in unstable soil)

Taller Tree
(likely to be toppled by wind unless staked)

Proper Staking Procedures

It is best not to stake a young tree. However, young trees whose tops are large in proportion to their root-balls may need extra support until the root system develops. Trees that have been previously grown with stakes in nursery fields also may need extra support until they are established.

There are lots of materials available for tying trees, including elastic webbing and stiff wire covered with pieces of old garden

hose. Whichever you use, make sure it contacts the tree with a broad surface to minimize rubbing. Wrap the tie around the tree trunk so that it forms a loose loop, and attach it firmly to the stake. Wrap a second tie around the trunk, and attach it to the second stake. Tie the tree loosely to avoid girdling as the trunk grows and to allow it some movement between the two stakes.

You should be able to unstake a tree at the end of the first growing season. Untie deciduous trees after their leaves have fallen to see whether they can stand on their own. Wait until just before new growth

begins in spring to unstake evergreen trees. If a tree still needs support, restake it and try again after the second growing season.

Very large trees may need anchoring until the roots grow into the parent soil. You can create a tripod support by attaching three guy wires that radiate out at approximately equal distance from the tree. Guys with springs for flexibility speed the ability of the tree to stand alone. The springs should have stops to give positive support in strong winds but provide flexibility in gentler winds.

Tree and Shrub Care

Trees and shrubs require little care once they are established. However, a bit of extra care while they are young will help them grow strong.

Water

Newly planted trees and shrubs need to be watered more frequently than established plants. How often plants should be watered and for how long will depend on many factors, including the water requirements of the specific plant, local rainfall, local temperatures, and the type of soil. To check whether the soil is dry, burrow an inch or two into the soil with your finger. If the soil feels dry, it's time to water. It won't take long, however, for you to get a sense of how frequently new trees and shrubs need watering based on the specific conditions in your garden.

If your soil is sandy, you'll need to water more often but for a shorter time. Clay soil remains moist much longer than sandy soil, but the water is prone to run off before it soaks in. If you are watering plants in heavy soil, let the hose run slowly for a longer time.

Shallow watering is damaging to trees and shrubs, encouraging them to grow shallow roots. Water deeply to stimulate growth of deep roots, which increase a plant's ability to absorb nutrients and tolerate dry spells. To ensure that the water goes deep into the ground, build a berm about 6 inches high around the drip line (the farthest reach of branches) of the tree or shrub to create a basin for the plant. When you water, simply fill the basin.

Mulch

Mulch newly planted trees and shrubs to slow the growth of weeds, hold in soil moisture, and keep the roots cool. Organic materials, such as dried grass clippings, straw, shredded leaves, cocoa bean hulls, and shredded bark, improve the soil while they keep weeds under control. If you mulch with fresh grass

clippings, spread the grass in thin layers and gradually top up to the recommended 4 to 6 inches as each new layer of grass dries out to avoid having slimy, rotted mulch. Pile organic mulch 4 to 6 inches deep and 4 to 6 inches from the trunk.

Fertilizer

Young plants benefit from a nutritional boost. Your best option is to topdress yearly with compost or aged manure. In addition to providing a slow, constant source of many nutrients, compost and aged manure improve the soil's structure. If you are using commercially prepared chemical fertilizers, the best time to feed is in the spring and early fall. Follow the directions on the package for the amount to give each plant.

Proper Care for Thriving Plants

Trees and shrubs form the backbone of your landscape, as mentioned at the beginning of this chapter. If you've chosen the plants wisely and given them extra care early on, they will reward you with nearly maintenance-free lives. While it is not impossible to move established trees and shrubs, it is not as easy to move a tree as it is to rearrange your perennial border. So take the time now to prepare the site, buy healthy stock, water, and fertilize to get your new plants well established. Years from now, when you are enjoying the stately presence of a mature tree or shrub in your landscape, you will be glad you gave the plant the extra attention it needed when it was new.

Inorganic mulches (counterclockwise from upper left) include gray granite (A), yellow beach pebbles (B), crushed red brick (C), crushed marble (D), light brown lava (E), red lava (F), and "jade" beach stones (G). The organic mulches include aged hardwood chips (H), fresh hardwood chips (I), red-dyed shredded cedar (J), shredded cedar (K), western pine-bark nuggets (L), shredded pine bark (M), shredded hemlock (N), pine needles (O), and shredded cypress (P).

chapter 5
lawns

Adding Lawns and Ground Covers

If trees and shrubs are the bones of a landscape, lawns and ground covers are the foundation. Sweeping oceans of lawn give a grounding and sense of space to a property. They are also a quick way to turn bare ground into a growing and functional part of the landscape. Ground covers add a lush presence and a sense of depth and richness. Within the wide range of plants suitable for ground covers, many can adapt to difficult growing situations, such as dry shade, while providing a pleasing alternative to bare ground.

This chapter is full of design ideas to get the most out of lawns and ground covers in your garden. In addition, you'll find valuable information for caring for the plants and preventing pests and diseases. With care and planning, your garden floor can be an outstanding feature, laying the foundation for the rest of the landscape.

Planning a Lawn

In many home landscapes, the lawn is there by default to cover bare ground rather than to provide an accent as a deliberately designed landscape feature. To really make the most of your lawn, put some thought into its design so that it becomes an emerald jewel in your garden. It is best to start by making a list of all the activities that will take place on the lawn. A large lawn might be used by your kids as a play space. The patch of lawn located under a shade tree can be the ideal spot for relaxing with a good book. Or the lawn could play a part in the arrangement of flower borders and gardens. You might, for example, surround a small lawn with beds of scented flowers and shrubs to create an intimate, fragrant spot. You can use a lawn to provide horizontal relief in a garden with lots of vertical elements, such as arbors and

trellises. Use narrow strips of lawn as soft pathways between different parts of the garden. When you are planning your landscape, think of the role you want the lawn to play in the overall look of the garden. Devote as much time to planning your green spaces as you do planning flower, tree, and shrub placement.

The Best Grass for You?

The ideal lawn grass is fine-textured and a deep, rich green. It should grow in a dense mat to keep out weeds.

It should also send its roots deep into the soil to grow vigorously and to withstand drought. However, there is no one all-purpose grass that does well throughout the country and meets all different needs. You should research the best lawn grasses for your area just as you would study which trees, shrubs, and perennials are the best to plant.

Grasses for Cool and Warm Seasons. There are more than 40 different kinds of grass for home gardens. They are divided into two main categories: cool-season and warm-season. Cool-season grasses are appropriate for regions where temperatures go below freezing during the winter months. They grow best in spring and fall, going dormant in winter and during spells of hot, dry summer weather. Warm-season grasses are ideal for the mild climates of the southern third of the country; they require less water than most cool-season grasses. They go dormant and turn brown in winter. When selecting, consider the amount of sun the area gets, foot traffic, the soil quality, and the amount of water available.

Lawns play an important role in the overall landscape of your yard. Here a patch of lawn provides a green open space among the heavily planted borders.

Sun-Loving Plant. In the wild you find grass growing in open meadows where sunlight is plentiful. There are a few varieties bred to grow in some shade, but even these require at least a few hours of daily sunlight and do even better if the shade is relatively bright. (See opposite.) To reduce the amount of shade for lawns, you can prune lower tree branches (or limb them up) to allow more light to reach the ground.

Heavy Foot Traffic. If you have children who will be running and playing on the lawn, select a sturdy variety such as perennial rye, tall fescue, Bermudagrass, Bahiagrass, or zoysia. Lawns growing in seaside gardens need to be salt tolerant. In northern climates the cool-season fescues tolerate salty air; try St. Augustinegrass in southern regions.

Difficult Soil Conditions

Other grasses are well suited to difficult soil conditions. Bahiagrass is adapted to southern coastal areas and will grow in sandy, infertile soil. Buffalograss is suited to the heavy clay soils found in western Louisiana, north-central Texas, eastern Colorado, western Kansas, Nebraska, and Oklahoma. In addition, it is extremely drought tolerant, surviving on as little as 12 inches of rain a year. It also requires minimal mowing because its natural height is only 3 to 4 inches. For acidic soil, plant Canada bluegrass, chewings fescue, or hard fescue. Perennial ryegrass, wheatgrass, and Bermudagrass all adapt to alkaline soil conditions.

Some of the grasses, such as Bermudagrass, are invasive, spreading horizontally in an aggressive manner. If you have flower beds or a shrub border next to a lawn that includes Bermudagrass, plan to use a sturdy metal or plastic edging to help keep the spreading grass in the lawn and out of the beds.

Buffalograss (left) thrives in hot, dry climates and only occassionally needs watering or mowing. **Bermudagrass** (right) also tolerates sun, heat, and drought. However, it is invasive and needs frequent edging.

This small lawn has a beautifully manicured edge clean cut with a straight-edge spade or edging tool. The enclosed grass lawn is set in the center of an encircling border of perennials, annuals, and shrubs.

Bare spots in the patch of sparse grass shown below have been worn by heavy foot traffic. Dense turf crowds out weeds and withstands traffic better.

Grasses that Grow In the Shade

Following is a list of cool- and warm-season grasses that tolerate shade. Recommended cultivars are listed after the hardiness zones.

Cool-Season Turf Grasses

■ Fine fescue (Chewings, *Festuca rubra* variety *commutata*; creeping red, *F. rubra* variety *rubra*; and Hard fescue, *F. longifolia*), Zones 1–6, 'Aurora', 'Jamestown II', 'Reliant', 'Scaldis', 'SR3100', 'SR5000', SR5100'

■ Kentucky bluegrass (*Poa pratensis*), Zones 1–6, 'A34', 'Georgetown', 'Glade'

■ Perennial ryegrass (*Lolium perenne*), Zones 4–6, 'Advent', 'APM', 'Express', 'Fiesta II', 'Manhattan II', 'Palmer II', 'SR4000', 'SR4100', 'SR4200'

■ Tall fescue (*Festuca elatior*), Zones 5–7, 'Apache', 'Arid', 'Bonanza II', 'Duster', 'Mustang', 'Pixie', 'Rebel Jr.', 'SR8200', 'Tomahawk'

Kentucky bluegrass (*Poa pratensis*)

Perennial ryegrass (*Lolium perenne*)

Tall fescue (*Festuca elatior*)

Warm-Season Turf Grasses

■ Bahiagrass (*Paspalum notatum*), Zones 9–11, 'Argentine', 'Pensacola'

■ Centipedegrass (*Eremochloa ophiuroides*), Zones 8–9, common, 'Oaklawn', 'Tennessee Hardy', Centennial'

■ St. Augustinegrass (*Stenotaphrum secundatum*), Zones 9–11, common, 'Bitterblue', 'Floralawn', 'Floratine', 'Raleigh'

■ Zoysia (*Zoysia species*), Zones 8–9, 'Belair'

Bahiagrass (*Paspalum notatum*)

Centipedegrass (*Eremochloa ophiuroides*)

Zoysiagrass (*Zoysia*)

Inexpensive or budget-priced seed is likely to have a low germination rate and contain a high proportion of weed seeds and inert matter or filler. Because these "cheap" packages contain so little that will actually grow, the real cost per pound often is higher than more expensive seed.

Read the package label carefully. Be sure that the seed is dated for the current year, and look for a guarantee of at least 85 percent germination and no more than 0.5 percent weed seeds. Make sure the label specifically states no noxious weed seed. Also look for a low percentage of annual grasses—no more than 3 to 5 percent. While annual rye is useful for overseeding warm-season lawns for winter green, it is not appropriate in a permanent lawn mixture because it dies after one season.

Today's grass has been bred for better long-term performance, disease resistance, deeper roots, and general attractive appearance. Look for trade or variety names rather than the generic name, such as Kentucky bluegrass. Don't buy the seed labeled VNS, which means Variety Not Stated. For cool-season grasses, look for a mixture that has been blended to meet specific growing requirements such as sun or shade, wet or dry, rich or poor soil, heavy or light traffic. According to The Lawn Institute (Marietta, Georgia), warm-season grasses should not be mixed. Most spread by stolons, and therefore instead of blending into a pleasing whole, they tend to form

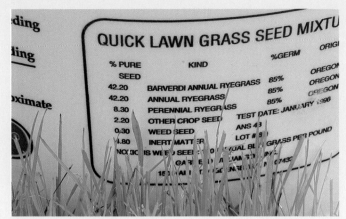

Grass seed package labels are required by law to provide information about seed content including germination rates, the date the seeds were tested, and percentage of different types of seed in the blend.

patches of distinct varieties. The Lawn Institute recommends choosing one particular turf grass among the warm-season grasses, one that will best adapt to your geographic area and particular lawn conditions.

If you are planting fescue or perennial rye, choose a seed mixture that contains at least 50 percent endophyte-enhanced seed. This seed is treated with fungi that kill many insects, including chinch bugs, billbugs, armyworms, aphids, and sod webworms. The fungi survive only about 9 months, so be sure the seed is fresh.

Chinch bug

Sod webworm

Japanese beetle grub

How Much Seed to Use for New Lawns

Seed Type	Kentucky Bluegrass	Tall Fescue	Perennial Ryegrass	Fine Fescue
Pounds per 1,000 square feet	2–3	5–7	4–6	4

Note: Setter spreadings may vary with type and model of spreader. Consult your owner's manual for exact settings. Apply 50 percent more seed if you are attempting to sow a new lawn in the spring.

Before planting a new lawn, send soil samples to a laboratory for an analysis of its components. (See Chapter 2, pages 13–17 for detailed information on soil tests.) The results will tell you whether you need to add any fertilizer, lime, gypsum, or sulfur to the soil before you plant. While you are waiting for the results, clean up the area, removing any debris, stones, stumps, or leftover building materials.

Amend the Soil. Using the results of your soil analysis as a guide, add whatever amendments are necessary to make the soil a suitable host for the grass seed. If you are committed to using a minimum of chemicals to keep your lawn robust and free of weeds, spend time and money now building the soil before you plant. Grass growing in deep, rich soil will be less vulnerable to pests and diseases, and less likely to need chemical treatments to solve those problems. It will grow vigorously, choking out weeds before they get a foothold, thus eliminating the need for chemical weed killers. Top-quality soil is the foundation of organic gardening; it will also make nonorganic lawns grow better and look better.

When you amend the soil, add a fertilizer high in phosphorus (such as 15-30-15) at a rate of 2 to 3 pounds per 1,000 square feet to help the new lawn establish a good root system. Till the soil to a depth of 4 to 6 inches to incorporate the amendments and to make it easier for the new roots to penetrate.

Eliminate the Weeds. After you've prepared the soil, you should eliminate the weeds and weed seed already present in the soil. A month before you plan to sow the grass seed, water the area regularly to encourage any seeds present to sprout. When they begin to grow, dislodge them with gentle tilling. Don't till too deeply, or you'll bring new weed seeds to the surface. While this step delays getting the lawn started by four weeks, it will make a major difference in successfully establishing a weed-free lawn. You can skip this step if you are laying sod; weed seeds won't sprout under the thick mats.

Grade the Site. If necessary, grade the site. Mowing steep slopes is difficult. In hilly situations where you don't want to grade, consider planting a low-maintenance ground cover over the slope rather than grass. Small dips and hummocks are also hard to mow; level these before planting to minimize scalping bumps with the lawn mower. Rake the area to smooth the soil and to remove any extra rocks and debris that were unearthed by the tiller. At the same time, fill in any low spots where water might pool, and create a pleasing, smooth surface. Finally, broadcast the seed, lay the sod, or plant the sprigs or plugs.

You will need a wide metal landscape rake, rototiller or shovel, high-phosphorous fertilizer and/or soil amendments, hose or sprinkler, grass seed, sod, plugs, or sprigs.

1. Work in Amendments. Till fertilizer, lime, and organic matter or other soil amendments into the soil. Follow the recommendations from the soil test for amounts and types of amendments needed.

2. Water the Area. Mist the area to be planted with a fine spray, and look for where puddles form. After the ground dries, fill any areas that puddled with soil taken from high spots.

3. Make Minor Grade Adjustments. A wide metal landscape rake is the ideal tool to level the surface and remove any loose stones. A smooth lawn is easier to maintain than one with bumps.

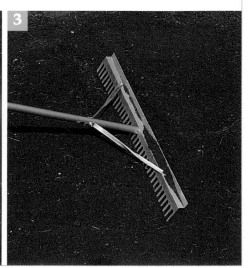

In addition to being less expensive than sod or even plugs and sprigs, seed provides a better choice of new high-quality cultivars. You can choose the grass type that will do best in your specific garden. However, it takes about a month for a newly seeded lawn to fill in, and several months for it to be durable enough for heavy use. In the meantime, there is a risk that the seed will wash away or be eaten by birds and that weeds will grow along with the grass.

Warm-season grasses germinate best when the soil is warm, between 70° and 90°F. To ensure a speedy and high rate of germination, wait to sow grass seed until late spring or early summer. Don't wait too long, however, or you'll risk giving the newly sown grass too short a growing season.

Late summer or early autumn, when the weather is cooling, is ideal for sowing (or overseeding) cool-season lawns. Cooler temperatures stimulate the germination process, and the autumn rains will relieve you of some of the watering chores. In northern climates, some people overseed their cool-season lawns in spring to fill in bare or thin patches and to improve the overall vigor of the lawn. Although possible, success is harder to achieve at that time of year. You must water faithfully until the grass is well-rooted and hope that the weather stays cool long enough so that summer heat doesn't damage young, tender roots.

Scatter the grass seed evenly over the soil. If you spread by hand, walk in one direction first, then walk perpendicular across the lawn to ensure full coverage. If you use a spreader, set it to release the grass seed at the rate recommended on the package label.

Once the seed is spread, rake lightly over the surface to scratch it into the soil, but don't bury it too deeply. All you really want to do is make good contact between the seed and the soil. Then lightly spread organic mulch, such as compost or straw, over the area to help keep the seed moist. Use a fine water spray to thoroughly moisten both grass seed and ground. Grass seed must continually be kept moist until it has germinated. If the weather is hot and dry the first week, you may need to water as frequently as three times a day. Once the roots start growing, you can back off to daily watering until the lawn looks strong.

Rope off the seeded area to discourage people and animals from walking across. If seed-eating birds are a problem, try tying strips of torn sheets or rags on the rope at regular intervals. They'll frighten the birds when they flap in the breeze. Don't mow a newly seeded lawn for at least four to six weeks. If you mow any sooner, you'll risk tearing up the shallow-rooted grass plants.

1. Spread the Seed. Aim for coverage of between 15 to 20 seeds per square inch after you've crossed the lawn twice with the spreader.

2. Rake the Seeded Surface. Rake lightly to mix the seed into the top ⅛ in. of soil. The raking can also disperse seed that was spread too thickly.

3. Nurture the Young Plants. Keep newly sprouted grass moist, watering twice a day if there is no rain. Maintain this level of moisture until the plants are 2 in. tall.

How to Overseed a Bare Patch

Lawns occasionally develop bare patches, which should be repaired so that they do not detract from the look of the rest of the lawn. Bare spots can easily be fixed by overseeding, a process similar to seeding, except in a smaller area. In the North, the best time to overseed is in late summer and ealy fall; in the South the recommended time is spring or early summer. Before you begin, choose an appropriate seed as discussed on pages 63–64. First roughen the surface with the rake. Then spread the seed with your hand or a spreader.

1. Loosen the Soil. To repair a bare patch of lawn, use a pitchfork to loosen the soil in the bare spot to a depth of 6 to 8 inches.

2. Level the Soil. Drag the flat end of a landscape rake over the patch to level the planting surface and remove all debris.

3. Spread the Seed. With your hand, evenly spread a mixture of seed, fertilizer, and soil over the affected area.

4. Tamp the Seeds Down. Use the flat end of the rake to tamp the seeds into the soil, or roll with a one-third full roller.

Sod is strips of growing lawn that have been cut out of the ground. Although more expensive than sowing a lawn from seed or plugs, sod provides instant coverage. When you order sod, have it delivered when it can be laid immediately. Even a few hours in the sun can damage the grass.

First, moisten the ground where you plan to put the sod. Then lay the sod, butting ends of adjoining strips together but not overlapping them. Work from the sodded area to the open soil. To protect the already-laid sod from excess foot traffic, place a plywood sheet over the surface while you are working.

Tamp down the soil to ensure that the roots make good contact with the soil, and then water thoroughly. The traditional way to tamp sod is to roll a water-filled roller over it.

Water within 30 minutes of laying the sod. Irrigate daily for the first ten days; then back off to every second or third

1. Cut the Sod into Pieces. Use a sharp trowel to cut sod to fit at butt joints or when cutting against a straightedge. You may also use the trowel to level any irregularities in the soil.

2. Lay the Sod. It's important to have full strips at the perimeter; narrow strips dry out faster than wide ones. As you lay the sod, keep all joints as tight as possible, but avoid overlapping or stretching the sod.

3. Fit Sections Together. When fitting two pieces of sod at an odd angle, lay one piece over the other, and cut through both at once. Then lift the top piece, and remove the waste underneath.

4. Cut the Last Piece to Fit. After you have laid sod to the opposite side of the area you're working in, cut the next-to-last piece to fit. Before cutting, roll out the sod for a test fit.

day until the new roots are well developed. It should take from two to four weeks for the sod to become properly established. After that, water slowly and deeply so that the water penetrates at least 6 inches into the soil. This method will encourage a deep root system that is more drought-tolerant than shallow-rooted grass. (See "Deep Watering," on page 74 to determine how long to water for best results.)

5. **Roll the New Sod Lawn.** If necessary, use an edger to trim between the edge of the sod and the bed. Then use a water-filled roller to eliminate air pockets and ensure that the roots make good contact with the soil.

6. **Clean Up Any Remaining Soil.** Fill the joints between strips with fine soil. Use a small, flexible rake to work any excess soil into the cracks between pieces of sod. Always stand on the board to protect planted areas.

Grass sprigs should be planted so that the top one-quarter of each plant is exposed. Grass sprigs can be broadcast at a rate of 5 to 10 bushels per 1,000 square feet or planted in furrows 1 to 2 inches deep.

How to Plant Plugs and Sprigs

An inexpensive alternative to sod is sprigs or plugs of grass. Warm-season grasses that spread readily—Bermuda, centipede, St. Augustine, and zoysia—are available as sprigs and plugs. Plugs are small strips or cubes of sod. Sprigs are individual grass plants or runners. Generally the plugs are sold in trays or flats of 12 or 24. Sprigs are usually sold by the bushel. In most cases you should plan for 4 to 5 bushels of grass sprigs per 1,000 square feet of lawn.

Plant the plugs or sprigs as you would any small plant, spacing them at recommended intervals. Bermudagrass plugs should be put in 4 to 12 inches apart. Centipedegrass, St. Augustinegrass, and zoysiagrass plugs all can be planted 6 to 12 inches apart. To save money, put them a little farther apart; for quicker coverage, put them closer together.

Grass plugs can be planted in furrows 6 to 12 inches apart or in individual holes. You can make your own plugs from unwanted areas of turf. Use a golf-green cup cutter for circular plugs or a sharp knife to cut square plugs.

Thatch is an accumulation of grass stems, stolons, rhizomes, roots, and leaves in the lawn that have not decomposed. It is more common in lawns with grasses that have stoloniferous roots running above ground such as bent grass, Bermudagrass, St. Augustinegrass, and zoysiagrass. Overfertilized grasses (especially those treated with concentrated, fast-acting synthetic fertilizers) are also more prone to develop thatch. Proper mowing (cutting off no more than one-third of the grass at one time) and fertilizing (not giving the lawn too much nitrogen, or using a slow-release formula) will help reduce the likelihood of thatch buildup. Also, aerate the lawn at least once a year. (See opposite.) For lawns that develop thick thatch no matter what you do, experts

recommend dethatching every three to five years. Topdressing with organic matter (ideally compost, which supplies organisms that break down thatch) is the best way to reduce thatch in the long run. Dethatching doesn't do anything to improve the soil or prevent future thatch buildup.

You may want to rent a power rake to remove the thatch and weeds. Set the blades to penetrate the thatch layer plus the top ¼ inch of soil. Run the machine back and forth in rows going in one direction, and then repeat the process, covering the ground from another angle. Water the lawn throughly to stimulate fresh growth. If you are seeding, keep the grass seed moist until it sprouts.

1. Analyze the Severity of the Problem. Dig up some lawn. Short roots, such as these, can result from excess thatch buildup.

2. Measure the Thatch. Roll back the grass. Thatch of more than ½ in. thick hinders water and amendments from reaching roots.

3. Dethatch the Lawn. Some grasses naturally produce more thatch. A healthy population of earthworms breaks down thatch.

Rennovating a Lawn

Over the years a lawn may begin to look ragged, especially if it isn't cared for properly. If more than half your lawn is full of weeds, has large worn-out or bare spots, or is rough and bumpy, consider replanting the entire area. Strip off the existing grass with a spade, working the blade in horizontal thrusts to cut through the roots. If the lawn is extensive, it may be more efficient and easier on your back to rent a sod-cutting machine. When the old grass is removed, prepare the soil

as shown on page 65, and replant.

In most cases you can renovate an existing lawn, rather than starting over. The best time of year to renovate a lawn is autumn or spring, when cooler weather and more frequent rains will promote regeneration.

The first step is to determine the source of the problem. Patchy, yellowed lawns are frequently the result of thatch buildup or soil compaction. Thatch is a light brown layer of grass debris that builds up just above the soil surface. Eventually it forms a dense mat that

stops water and fertilizer from penetrating the soil. As a result, the lawn languishes. Compacted soil, caused by heavy traffic (especially when the soil is very wet) also keeps water and oxygen from penetrating the soil, starving and suffocating the grass roots. Cut out a 3-inch section of lawn, and study the cross section. If the thatch is more than ½ inch thick or the soil is compacted, you'll need to take remedial action. Both dethatching and aerating are best done before you spread any seed, fertilizer, or amendments.

Aerate

There are special forks and shoes with prongs designed to penetrate the ground to aerate the grass. While wearing the shoes, walk around the lawn, punching holes as you step. The forks and shoes that remove plugs are fine for a small lawn, but the most efficient and effective way to do the job on a large lawn is to use an aerating machine. Look for the kind that actually lifts out the cores of soil. These machines are available at outdoor equipment rental stores. Crisscross over the lawn in different directions to thoroughly work the space. Lawns growing in heavy clay soil will need aerating more often than those growing in sandy soil or loam. Aerating lawns growing in clay soils when they're wet will cause compaction rather than improvement.

Replant

Begin by mowing the lawn as close to the ground as possible. Then use a dethatching machine or power rake (available from equipment rental stores) to break up the grass. Run the machine back and forth in rows going in one direction; then repeat, covering the same territory from a different angle. Continue passing over the area until the grass is well broken up and the soil surface is exposed between the remaining grass plants. Rake off the excess debris.

If a soil test recommends lime or sulfur to adjust soil pH, spread it over the lawn now. If you aren't using lime, you can fertilize now. Don't spread fertilizer at the same time that you spread lime, or a chemical reaction will cause the nitrogen to evaporate; wait a few weeks. Wait until after you seed to spread topdressings of compost or aged manure.

Select a blend or mixture of named, improved varieties of lawn seed. Look for ones that match your growing conditions (sun, shade, or high-traffic). Insect and disease resistance, stress tolerances, and sufficient vigor to crowd out weeds are other factors to consider.

Because you are going to all this trouble, you want to be sure to plant a seed variety that you know is an improvement over the common older varieties. Sow the seed using a drop or broadcast spreader. You can plug grasses that spread with runners (St. Augustine, zoysia, Bermuda, and buffalo) directly into the renovated lawn. Water the newly seeded lawn frequently to keep the seed moist but not overly wet until it sprouts.

If you are overseeding a warm-season lawn with annual rye for a green winter lawn, simply mow the existing lawn as short as possible, rake off clippings and thatch, spread the seed, and water to keep the seed continuously moist until it sprouts. This technique also works for areas of lawn that are a bit thin but not too weedy.

A manual aerator does the job well, but slowly. Step down on the aerator every few inches as you walk across the lawn. Special aerating shoes with prongs are easier to use.

An aerating machine (above) is the best way to do the job. Long, slim corers (left) scoop out plugs of the soil's top layer (right) and deposit them on the surface, where they eventually break down to feed the grass.

Types of Nitrogen Fertilizer

Slow-Release	Advantages	Disadvantages
Sulfur-coated urea Bone meal Dried poultry waste Soybean meal Composted manure Alfalfa meal	Nitrogen released gradually; low incidence of burning; fewer applications used; lasts longer	Higher initial costs; dependent on warm weather for release; takes longer for turf grass response

Fast-Release	Advantages	Disadvantages
Ammonium nitrate Calcium nitrate Ammonium phosphate Ammonium sulfate Urea	Immediate nitrogen availability; generally costs less; better known release rate; releases even in cold weather	More apt to leach; more apt to burn foliage; more frequent applications required; may acidify soil; may make plants vulnerable to disease; requires more frequent watering

Maintenance Guide

Grass is probably the highest-maintenance plant in a garden. It requires weekly mowing during the growing season, edging, trimming, fertilizing, and watering. Nevertheless, by following a few basic principles for a care regimen, you can grow a healthy, beautiful lawn.

Feed and Weed

Poor soil leaves a lawn looking thin and weedy. Too much fertilizer also causes problems, making the lawn prone to thatch buildup as well as insects and disease. The ideal for the health of your lawn and your budget is to use the minimum amount of fertilizer necessary to keep the grass looking healthy and green.

Your goal is to provide enough nutrients to encourage a strong root system that will support healthy top growth. The best way to fertilize a lawn is to use slow-release nitrogen. Homeowners who spread quick-release nitrogen in large quantities on their lawn for an instant rich, green effect do more damage than good. The lush leaf growth will occur at the expense of the roots, creating thatch and weakening the overall plant. Also, those lawns will need much more frequent mowing.

The quick-fix nitrogen fertilizers most commonly used are ammonium nitrate and ammonium sulfate. They are less expensive than the slower-acting fertilizers, making them attractive to budget-conscious gardeners. However, they can be more costly in the long run. Quick-release nitrogen is designed to dissolve easily, but that means a heavy downpour may wash much of it out of the soil and off your lawn. Slow-release forms of nitrogen include sulfur-coated urea, resin-coated urea, urea formaldehyde, and organic fertilizers such as Milorganite. While these are more expensive up front, they do not have to be applied as often. As a rule, lawns fed with a slow-release form of nitrogen have better color and thickness and more reduced leaf growth than lawns treated with quick-release nitrogen.

Organic Fertilizers. More and more gardeners are opting for organic fertilizers that boost the lawn without damaging the environment. You'll need to use the organics in larger quantities than chemical fertilizers. However, with organic fertilizers, you are incorporating organic material into the soil in addition to feeding. This builds the quality of the soil and provides longer-term benefits than are provided by quick-acting, concentrated fertilizers.

When to Fertilize

The best time to fertilize a lawn is when it is actively growing.

- Cool-season grasses grow best in spring and fall, so fertilize cool-season grasses at the beginning of the growing season in spring or as cooler temperatures return in fall.

- If you plan to fertilize at regular intervals over a period of months in spring, stop as soon as the weather gets hotter. If you like, you can feed once more in autumn after the first frost to set up the lawn for next spring's growth.

- Feed warm-season grasses in late spring and again in August.

- If you are using a slow-release form of nitrogen, feed smaller doses every six to ten weeks until about eight weeks before the first frost date.

- If the lawn has good color and is growing well, delay additional feedings by a week or two.

- Overfeeding a lawn is wasteful and damaging to the environment. Excess fertilizer may be leached out by watering and carried into underground water systems

Other Lawn Boosters. In addition to fertilizers, substances called biostimulants have recently become available. These compounds increase the grasses' ability to absorb important nutrients from the soil, thus improving growth and increasing resistance to pests and diseases. One product called Mycor contains mycorrhizal fungi. It works to create a favorable environment for nitrogen-fixing bacteria in the soil and improves the grasses' ability to take in nutrients through their roots. Another product, BioPro, contains peat derivatives and micronutrients. It provides three benefits to lawns: improvment of the structure, increase in the plant's ability to use available nitrogen, and introduction of organic material to the soil. Compost and seaweed products are also sources of biostimulants. Talk to an experienced nurseryman to find out what organic options are available in your community.

An easy way to add extra nutrients to your lawn is to leave the clippings in place when you mow. Contrary to popular wisdom, these clippings do not build up a layer of thatch. If you mow before the grass gets too long so the clippings aren't left in large clumps that block light to the grass, the clippings will quickly decompose, adding organic matter to the soil as well as nutrients. A mulching mower is a great asset because it chops up the grass into little pieces that can decompose quickly. Decomposing grass clippings also encourage earthworms, which aerate the soil and add to the nutrient content with their castings. Instead of throwing your clippings away, leave them on the lawn. The clippings can reduce the need for fertilization by as much as 25 percent, helping your lawn and the environment.

Weed Control. A healthy lawn will grow dense enough to crowd out weedy plants. Control any annual weeds that intrude simply by mowing. You'll remove the seed head before it matures, and the plant will die at the end of its growth cycle. Perennial weeds are more of a problem. If you have them in small quantities, hand-weed the lawn before they set seed, and work to remove each weed's entire root system. It's easiest to weed by hand when the soil is moist and soft. An easy way to remove weeds is to pour boiling water on them. This is especially effective when trying to remove weeds from between the cracks of a patio or on the edge of the lawn. Another option is to use a fertilizer in early spring that is mixed with a preemergent weed killer. Be aware, however, that this is a nonselective herbicide. It will kill grass seed as well as weed seeds.

Poison ivy grows in recently disturbed soil, such as in new lawns. The three red leaves are distinctive, but be aware that the leaves turn green as they mature.

Crabgrass is the bane of homeowners. Mowing high, removing seed heads, and maintaining dense turf are essential to control this common lawn weed.

Deep Watering

Lawns grow best when they are watered deeply and infrequently. The deep water penetration encourages roots to grow down, rather than sideways, improving the root structure and drought tolerance of the grass. If your soil is dense clay, water slowly so that the water can soak in rather than run off. The average lawn needs about 1 inch of water on a weekly basis. If your soil is a heavy clay, it can take as long as 5 hours for 1 inch of water to penetrate properly. At the other extreme, sandy soil will absorb 1 inch of water in approximately 10 minutes. To determine how much water you are delivering, space shallow cans at regular intervals along your lawn and time how long it takes them to fill. One inch of water will penetrate about 12 inches in sandy soil, 7 inches in loam, and 4 to 5 inches in clay. If you have clay soil and want to water the lawn to a depth of 6 inches, you would need to leave the sprinkler on until there is 1½ inches of water in each container. Ideally a lawn should be watered to a depth of 6 to 12 inches.

Water lawns early in the morning or late in the afternoon. It is generally less windy at those times of day, so the water won't blow into the air. The cooler temperatures and lack of wind also will minimize evaporation.

Proper Mowing

Many lawn problems are a result of cutting grass too short. Grass that is shorn too close is more likely to succumb to stresses caused by drought, insect injury, foot traffic, or inadequate sun. Ideally you should never remove more than one-third of the leaf surface each time you mow. See the table on the following page for guidelines on ideal heights for different grasses. The lawn's rate of growth—and therefore how often you need to mow—will depend on how warm the weather is, how much water the lawn has received, and whether you fertilized. Those factors will vary throughout the season, although most people find that a schedule of weekly mowing works well.

At least once a year you should sharpen your lawn mower blades. Blunt mower blades can ruin a lawn by tearing the leaves. Each torn blade will die back ⅛ to ¼ inch, giving the lawn a brown tinge. The ragged edge on each blade of grass also makes the lawn more susceptible to disease.

Lawns mowed to the proper height are typically healthier and better able to resist disease than grass cropped short. Keep the mower blades sharp, and follow the recommended mowing heights given on the next page.

Gill-over-the ground, also called ground ivy, spreads by aboveground stolons, shown here, and by underground rhizomes.

Purslane is a warm-season annual that thrives in hot, dry weather. Its fibrous roots are easy to pull, but new roots develop from stem fragments.

Today homeowners can choose from a variety of lawn mowers. Most of the newer models are mulching mowers, designed to pulverize the grass so that it breaks down quickly. When buying a mower, be sure the machine has a good warranty. Also check that it can be serviced at local shops and that parts are readily available. Once a year, have it tuned, cleaned, and serviced, and the blade sharpened; a good time is during the winter before the mowing season begins. Regular maintenance is a good long-range investment. The major mower types are described here.

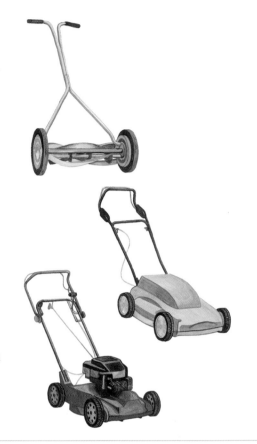

Reel Mower. The reel mower is the type with a cylinder of blades. Most have five blades, although for a finer cut (as on golf courses) there are seven- and nine-blade machines. There are gas-powered reel-style mowers, but most homeowners who select this option stick with the hand-push models. A reel-type hand mower is excellent for a small, level, and even lawn. It is compact to store, quiet to use, doesn't pollute, and in a small space takes no more time to do the job than a motorized mower.

Electric Mower. If you prefer a motorized mowing machine, the electric ones are ideal for small properties. They run quietly and are nearly maintenance-free. You can choose a cordless one that runs for an hour or more on a rechargeable battery, or opt for one with a long cord. In that case, take care that you don't run over the cord, cutting it along with the grass.

Gas-Powered Mower. Gas engines are often more powerful than electric motors, and they do not limit you by the length of the cord. There is a great range of gas mowers, including hand-propelled and self-propelled walk-behind designs as well as ride-on models for large properties. You can buy them with detachable bags for collecting the clippings and with mulchers that chop up the grass finely and spray it back onto the lawn. You will have a choice of horsepower, safety features, and starting features; you can choose a two-cycle engine, in which the oil is mixed with the gasoline, or a four-cycle engine, which runs on regular gasoline with a separate place for pouring in the oil. Gas-powered mowers need regular maintenance to run properly.

5 Lawns

Best Mowing Heights

Grass Type	Finished Height
Bluegrass	2 inches
Perennial ryegrass	2 inches
Tall fescue	2 inches
Fine fescue	2 inches
St. Augustinegrass	2 inches
Buffalograss	2 inches
Bermudagrass	1½ inches
Zoysiagrass	1½ inches
Centipedegrass	1½ inches

Source: The Lawn Institute (Marietta, Georgia)

Adjust the cutting height of the mower. By setting the mower to cut higher, you will reduce weed growth and slow the frequency of mowing. Short grass does not shade out weeds like taller grass, and its crown is exposed.

Adding Ground Covers

Ground covers are marvelous alternatives to lawns in garden areas that aren't subject to foot traffic. Ground covers add color and texture to the garden, and most don't require mowing or raking. Use them instead of grass around trees and shrubs to eliminate trimming, and in difficult areas where grass won't grow or mowing would be difficult.

Once established, most ground covers will block out weeds. Use ground covers to control erosion on steep slopes or to fill in space in beds until the slower growing plants mature.

Ground Covers Galore

Although many people think of ground covers as plants that hug the ground, almost any low-growing plant with a spreading habit is suitable for a ground cover. This includes small shrubs and conifers such as rockspray cotoneaster (*Cotoneaster horizontalis*) and creeping juniper (*Juniper horizontalis*). These shrubs grow as tall as 3 feet but cover the ground admirably. Rockspray cotoneaster provides three-season interest with small pink flowers in spring, glossy green foliage in summer, and red berries and foliage in autumn. Creeping juniper is a hardy plant that will grow in difficult situations where other plants won't survive, including steep slopes. It is an excellent choice for erosion control.

Vigorous clumping perennials such as daylilies also work well as ground covers; they are particularly useful on a steep slope because they require little care. Other perennials that cover the ground effectively if they are planted close together include lady's mantle (*Alchemilla mollis*), beach wormwood (*Artemisia stelleriana*), and showy sundrops (*Oenothera speciosa*). In addition to its silvery gray-green foliage, which catches water droplets and displays them like shiny jewels on velvet, lady's mantle produces pretty chartreuse blooms that combine well with blue flowers. As its name suggests, beach wormwood does well by the seaside in sandy soil. It grows up to 2 feet tall with a 3-foot spread. Showy sundrops, which tolerate drought, will grow happily in full sun or partial shade. Harsh, difficult conditions are a good way to keep them under control; in moist, fertile soil they will invade. They are easy to grow and reward gardeners with a pretty display of cup-shaped soft pink flowers in early summer.

Ferns that spread with underground runners are a lovely ground cover in shady areas, and fringed bleeding heart (*Dicentra eximia*) blooms in partial shade throughout most of the summer. Plant hostas close together in shady areas. Most can tolerate both wet and dry conditions.

Bright ground cover adds light (above). *Lamium maculatum* 'White Nancy' sparkles under the shade of a large conifer. Even when out of bloom, the silver leaves margined with green brighten the otherwise dark spot.

Foliage creates cover (right). *Phlox divaricata*, hosta, foamflower, ajuga, and sweet woodruff foliage intermingle compatibly on this shady slope. In due course, their foliage will mask the dying daffodil leaves.

A weed barrier, *Liriope muscari* 'Big Blue' grows in a dense mass, so weeds cannot invade (above). In autumn, violet blue flower spikes brighten the display. The evergreen grass grows 10 to 18 in. tall.

This shady woodland slope (right) has been planted with various hostas, ferns, and Siberian bugloss (*Brunnera macrophylla*), to create a varied, textured composition with little maintenance required.

Problem-Solving Ground Covers

Within the plant kingdom there are ground covers that will grow in almost any difficult spot in the garden. In a hot, dry garden, consider planting pussytoes (Antennaria dioica) or hardy iceplant (*Delosperma cooperi*). Choose crown vetch (*Coronilla varia*) or creeping juniper (*Juniperus horizontalis*) on steep, sunny slopes where mowing is difficult. If sandy soil and salt spray are a problem, look into growing rugosa rose, mondo grass (*Ophiopogon japonicus*), bearberry (Arctostaphylos uva-ursi), or creeping lilyturf (*Liriope spicata*).

Ivy will grow in deep, dry shade and in areas where there is little root room. Snow-in-summer (*Cerastium tomentosum*) will tolerate clay soil and loves a hot, sunny bank; if the soil is too good, however, the plant can become invasive. Pachysandra is happy competing with tree roots and makes a pretty, tailored green collar when planted around trees.

Grow an evergreen ground cover such as periwinkle (*Vinca minor*) over spring-flowering bulbs. The dark green periwinkle leaves make a pretty backdrop when the bulbs are in bloom; later they help disguise the dying leaves. Also, you won't risk disturbing the bulbs by digging about in the bed later in the season. Choose bulbs such as Narcissus varieties, whose flowers are tall enough to be visible above the vinca.

The obvious approach to ground covers is to massplant one species for uniform coverage. Another alternative is to intermingle different creeping plants with a variety of leaf and flower colors and textures to create a dazzling tapestry effect. For best success, mix plants that require similar growing conditions. For example, mix different varieties of creeping thyme, such as caraway-scented thyme (*Thymus Herba-barona*), with its dark green leaves and matting growth, golden lemon thyme (*T. x citriodorus 'Aurea'*), with its green and yellow variegated leaves, and silver thyme (*T. vulgaris 'Argenteus'*), with silver and green variegated leaves.

When selecting ground covers, choose ones that are suited to the soil and climate conditions in your garden. You'll be rewarded with minimal maintenance.

chapter 6
flowers

Plants for the Garden

Choosing the plants and imagining them in all their glory is perhaps the most satisfying aspect of planning a perennial bed or border. Garden design experts recommend combining at least three to five of each plant in clumps or drifts to create an impact.

Learn the mature heights of the plants. In a border you generally want the tallest plants in back so that all the plants can be seen, although you may move one or two forward to cast interesting shadows. Varied heights also increase the sense of depth in a border.

Color and Texture

Floral color is probably the most obvious feature of a bed or border. You can choose a color theme, such as a white garden, a red border, or a bed planted with pastel flowers. Remember that you don't have to be a slave to the concept. Think about introducing a pale lemon yellow flower to a blue garden to emphasize the blue flowers. Another idea, credited to the English gardener Gertrude Jekyll, is to gradually move through the color spectrum, making each section blend imperceptibly with the next. For example, a border that begins with yellow at one end could gradually move into the orange palette, followed by reds. A border that mixes colors throughout may be more to your taste.

Don't forget the value of gray foliage. Use it to create a restful spot in the midst of a lot of exciting color or as a buffer between two plants whose colors might clash. A large blob of white in a bed or border visually punches a hole in the design. Instead sprinkle white throughout to brighten the nearby colors and to add sparkle and life.

While designing your bed or border, also consider the shapes and textures of leaves and flowers. Aim to create an interesting rhythm throughout the bed or border.

When choosing plants for the bed or border, don't overlook shrubs,

Yellow and orange tickseed and lilies happily mingle with violet balloon flowers and pink snapdragons.

biennials, annuals, bulbs, and even small trees, particularly dwarf conifers. The trees and shrubs give year-round structure to the design. Many shrubs appropriate for perennial borders also produce flowers. Some give a lovely autumn display; others produce attractive berries or have pretty bark. Annuals provide continual color spots throughout the summer, and bulbs bring interest from early spring through autumn. Think of your border as a mixed border.

Frame the Bed with Edging Plants.
Like a picture on the wall, beds and borders generally look better if a

frame sets them off. Consider edging the border with a mixture of low-growing plants such as ageratum, sweet alyssum, santolina, or dianthus.

There are basic principles and guidelines for designing a mixed perennial border, and it's important to know the rules. However, each garden is a reflection of the owner's own taste and personality. So there is no need to be a slave to the rules. Be bold in experimenting with combinations of color, texture, and form. Nothing in a garden is permanent. No doubt your perennial bed will evolve as you gain more experience.

6 Flowers

A lush island bed in a small town garden brims with cannas, daylilies, hostas, and potted plants.

Adding Borders and Beds

Flowers touch our lives in a multitude of ways, soothing us with their scents and pleasing us with their delightful colors and forms. In the garden they bring sparkle, variety, and vibrancy.

Many gardens in North America are rich with floral interest in spring when so much is in bloom. Unfortunately, after the initial burst of color, some gardens quit, and for the rest of the growing season they are masses of unrelieved green. This lack of summer interest in the garden is unnecessary. Even in regions of the country where summers are the hottest and most humid, there are summer-blooming annuals, perennials, and bulbs that can grace the garden. All it takes is some thoughtful planning.

Designing Borders and Beds

Borders. Traditionally perennial borders follow the line of paths, enhancing the journey from one part of the garden to another with a wonderful floral display along the way. But there are many other places you could site a border. For example, in lieu of a fence, you could create a perennial border across the front of your property to define your private space. Mix shrubs with perennials against your home to transform a foundation planting into a mixed border. And you can line your driveway with perennial flowers.

Perennial borders generally look best against a background. Dark green hedges are a wonderful foil for flowers. Yew is often used as a formal background to a perennial border because it has finely textured foliage and a deep color that sets off other plants to advantage. If you prefer an informal planted background, consider a screen of tall ornamental grass or a mixed collection of unpruned shrubs. Other options for backgrounds to perennial borders include trellises and fences. Look around your garden. You might find that an appropriate backdrop for a perennial border already exists.

Beds. Although beds and borders frequently are referred to in the same breath, there is a difference. A bed is an island of plantings. You can walk around a bed, viewing it from all sides. You can make a bed as large or small as you like, but make sure it complements the scale of other features in your garden. Unless you include maintenance paths to access the interior of a large bed, make the bed small enough so you can reach to the center to look after plants.

Designing with Perennials

For many, the prospect of designing a perennial bed or border is fraught with uncertainty and anxiety. There is so much to coordinate—from plant heights, bloom times, and flower colors to care requirements and hardiness. A few simple techniques can help you create a perennial border.

Larry Griffith, a horticultural research associate at Colonial Williamsburg, Virginia, has devised a technique that removes the fear and mystique from the process of designing with perennials.

Gather Plants in Your Head

First, draw to scale an outline of the border on a piece of paper. Choose a scale that fits comfortably on the paper. For example, if your border is going to be 21 feet long and 6 feet wide, you could tape two standard 8½-by-11-inch sheets of paper together to have a 22-inch width of paper, making your scale 1 inch to 1 foot. Then draw a diamond grid pattern on the paper, spacing the lines to scale so that they are 2 to 4 feet apart in the actual bed. (See illustrations on page 82.)

Meanwhile, start brainstorming about which flowers you might like to have in the border. A plant catalog full of photographs will give you an idea of what various plants look like. Cross check with local nurseries to know what is available and what does well in your area. Write down more plants than you'll actually need.

Laying Out the Border

To design the border, you'll need to know the plant's projected height, the flower color, and the season of bloom. You easily can bring order to this information if you create a four-column chart. Run the plant names down the left column, and then create a column each for height, flower color, and bloom season. Now you can begin to put the jigsaw together. Start from the back of the border. Choose the tallest plants, and mark their proposed position in one of the diamond grids on the paper map. To help you visualize the color combinations you are creating, color the grid the approximate color of the flower. For a more natural look, plant clumps of flowers in drifts that blend into each other.

You may prefer a border that has moments of flower interest as you progress through the season or a border that knocks your socks off for a few weeks with a solid mass of bloom. In either case, put plants that will bloom about the same time with complementary flower colors near each other.

Also think about the shape of the flower. A perennial garden consisting only of blossoms with tall spires would be monotonous. Instead, mix spiky flower forms with round-headed flowers as well as others with cup formations and trumpet shapes.

When you've filled in the back space on the map, begin work on the middle section of the border. Select perennials of mid height, and mark their proposed position in the garden on the grid. The lowest-growing plants should be in front along the edges.

Repetition and rhythm are two features of a good garden design. You can introduce these elements to a long perennial border by repeating a basic design. If your border is long, divide it into thirds or quarters and repeat the same placement and combination of plants three or four times down the length.

You'll need patience with your design. A perennial border takes two to three years to come into its own. Your border should look a little thin the first year, with plenty of earth visible between the plants. But don't be tempted to fill in with more plants. You should space the plants far enough apart so that they have room to grow and spread to their mature sizes.

The perennial border at Barnsley House shows the beauty of using one dominant color sprinkled with dashes of another.

The plan view and the perspective view are two different ways to look at the same garden. The numbers on the plants, in the diamonds, and at the left of the table correspond to one another. On the plan view, notice how the colors overlap the edges of the diamonds like drifts, blending seamlessly. This plan is intended to be repeated in a mirror image down the border.

Speaking at a garden symposium in Virginia, Penelope Hobhouse explained the technique of creating repetition and rhythm in a border with a story about her friend and colleague, Rosemary Verey. The story was that Verey and another colleague had worked all morning choosing plants for a border. By lunchtime they had done one-quarter of the length. "Oh dear," lamented Verey's colleague, "this is taking longer than I thought. We've still got three-quarters of the border to do." To this Verey retorted, "Don't be silly. We're done. We'll just repeat this plan three times!"

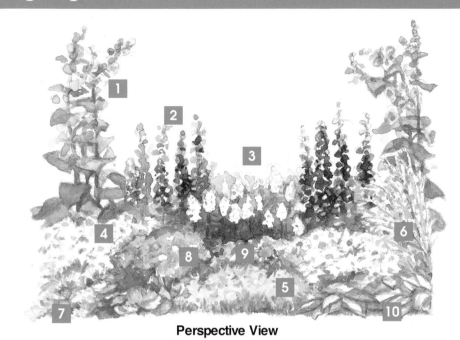

Perspective View

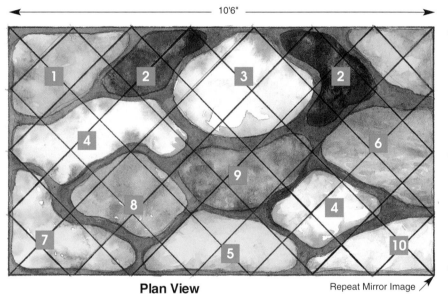

Plan View

Repeat Mirror Image ↗

Plant	Height and Spread	Season of Bloom	Hardiness Zone
1 *Alcea rosea* (common hollyhock)	60"–96"H x 24"W	Early and Mid Summer	Zones 3–9
2 D*elphinium* 'Bellamosum' (larkspur)	36"–48"H x 18"W	Early and Mid Summer	Zones 3–7
3 P*hlox paniculata* 'David' (phlox)	40"H x 40"W	Mid to Late Summer	Zones 4–8
4 *Leucanthemum x superbum* (shasta daisy)	30"H x 18"W	Early Summer and Fall	Zones 5–8
5 *Coreopsis verticillata* (tickseed)	24"–32"H x 18"W	Summer to Autumn	Zones 3–8
6 P*erovskia atriplicifolia* (Russian sage)	48"H x 36"W	Summer to Autumn	Zones 6–9
7 *Alchemilla mollis* (lady's mantle)	24"H x 30"W	Summer to Autumn	Zones 4–7
8 G*eranium* 'Johnson's Blue' (cranesbill)	18"H x 24"–30"W	Summer	Zones 4–8
9 *Scabiosa columbaria* (scabiosa)	16"H x 16"W	Mid to Late Summer	Zones 3–8
10 *Stachys byzantina* (lamb's ears)	18"H x 24"W	Summer to Autumn	Zones 4–8

Adding Annuals

True annuals are plants that complete their whole life cycle in one year. They grow, bloom, go to seed, and die. In nature's urge to propagate itself, annual plants will keep producing flowers if they are not allowed to set seed. This is why gardeners can enjoy such a long season of bloom from annuals.

Most of the plants we grow as annuals are frost-tender perennials that hale from warm climates such as Central and South America, South Africa, and the Mediterranean area. In fact, many of them are grown as perennials in the subtropical parts of southern California and south Florida. There, homeowners enjoy the perpetual blooms of impatiens and wax begonias 12 months of the year. They manage the plants by trimming them back when they get leggy to encourage bushy growth and intense flowering.

The great advantage of many annuals is that they flower generously throughout the growing season, providing dependable color and interest in the garden. In cold-season climates, you can plant annuals in spring and enjoy a continous display of flowers until they succumb to the first killing frost in autumn.

Because of their energetic propensity to stay in flower all season long, annuals are an excellent choice for creating dramatic container displays. Because they need to be replanted each spring, you also have the opportunity to renew the container soil annually.

Annuals in the Landscape

Annuals are also an asset in the perennial border. Most perennials bloom for just a few weeks a year. Even gifted perennial border designers struggle with planting combinations that will flower from spring through autumn. That's where annuals come in handy. They grow quickly, so you can plug them into holes in the border and use them to extend the beauty of the display if there's a gap in the bloom cycle of the perennials.

Annuals were all the rage in the Victorian era when many of today's popular plants were first brought back to Europe and England by plant explorers. Home gardeners delighted in creating mass displays of them and planted them in colorful strips or elaborate patterns with bold color combinations. The technique, called bedding out or carpet bedding, fell out of favor when influential English gardeners wrote scathing, disparaging descriptions of these annual arrays, referring to the "ingenious monstrosity" of carpet bedding. As a result, the fashion for carpet bedding died, gradually giving way to the labor-intensive perennial beds and borders. However, many municipalities and homeowners with less time and staff to garden create stunning visual displays, perhaps because they can produce an eye-catching, season-long display relatively easily and inexpensively.

Because so many annuals flower throughout the growing season, they are ideal for cutting gardens.

Annuals provide long color in the landscape. Shown here: ageratum and marigolds are still going strong in September.

This cutting garden of annuals includes marigolds and ageratum. Annuals produce more flowers if they are cut.

In fact, they benefit from being cut. With annuals, the more flowers you pick, the more the plants produce. Many annuals, such as zinnias, marigolds, and even impatiens, will last at least a week in a vase if they are picked fresh. Remove faded flowers promptly to encourage new blooms, as annuals stop blooming once they form seed. (See "Deadheading and Pinching," page 89.)

The purple iris (above left) sits among a golden ring of the perennial yellow ice plant.

Pale-pink forget-me-nots among hot-pink tulips create a stunning scene.

Yellow and pale-pink lily bulbs make an interesting display with goat's beard.

This container garden (above right) includes: yellow *Narcissus* (center) and *Viola* (front).

Designing with Bulbs

In Holland, bulbs are a spring garden staple. In North America, we love spring-blooming bulbs, but we rarely think of them as an important element in the garden design. We also often ignore bulbs that bloom at other times of the year. In addition to the traditional spring displays of tulips and daffodils, there are bulbs that bloom in summer or autumn—and a few, such as *Galanthus nivalis* (snowdrops), *Iris reticulata*, and *Eranthis hyemalis* (winter aconite), that bloom in late winter.

Many of the minor bulbs (so-called because they are smaller than tulips and daffodils) are low-growing, ideal in rock gardens. These include *Muscari* spp. (grape hyacinth), *Anemone blanda* (windflower), winter aconite, and hardy cyclamen. Midsize plants such as many daffodils and tulips mix well in perennial borders. Very tall bulb plants such as *Fritillaria imperialis* (crown imperial), lilies, and *Eremurus* spp. (foxtail lily) are a wonderful backdrop to other plantings and are useful as vertical accents in a border. Of course, massed in a bed on their own, a single variety of bulb or a

pleasing combination that blooms simultaneously makes a spectacular floral display. The disadvantage to such a massed display is the unsightly bulb foliage when the flowers are gone. One way of ameliorating the problem is to overplant the bulbs with annuals or a late-starting perennial such as hostas or daylilies in the bed with the bulbs. As the perennial grows, it will hide the dying bulb foliage.

Bulbs in Containers

Many bulbs also are ideal for containers because you can whisk the plants out of sight when they go through their unattractive dying-back stage. Pack as many as possible into each pot to obtain a full bouquet, and stick to one variety unless you are sure both will bloom at the same time. Plant bulbs in containers at the same time as your bulbs in the garden. Because most spring-flowering bulbs need a period of chilling to bloom well, pots of these bulbs should stay outdoors or in a cold place over winter. Keep the containers out of direct sunlight so that the soil remains cool. Otherwise, the warmed soil will trigger the bulbs to sprout before they have developed adequate root systems.

Plant Bulbs in Groups. Whether growing in pots or in garden beds, bulbs look better planted in tightly packed clumps of ten or more or in drifts that flow like rivers. Avoid buying fewer than 10 of any one bulb. Purchasing them in packages of 50 to 100 is even better. Brent Heath, owner of Brent and Becky's Bulbs (a mail-order bulb company in Virginia), recommends planting five large daffodil bulbs per square foot. That means a small garden plot just 5 feet square should be planted 125 daffodils! It takes even more small bulbs, such as crocuses, to fill a square foot. Arrange the bulbs so that they are grouped by color and type; if you want the display to peak all at once, mix varieties that bloom at the same time

Blooming Bulbs

Summer-Blooming Bulbs

Agapanthus africanus and cultivars (African lily)
Allium caeruleum
Allium christophii (star of Persia)
Allium giganteum
Amaranthus x Amarcrinum memoria-corsii
Begonia Tuberhybrida Hybrids (tuberous begonia)
Canna x generalis and cultivars (canna lily)
Crocosmia cultivars (montbretia)
Dahlia cultivars
Gladiolus cultivars
Lilium species and cultivars (lily)
Lycoris squamigera (magic lily)
Tulbaghia violacea (society garlic)
Zantedeschia aethiopica (calla lily)
Zephyranthes grandiflora (zephyr lily)

Autumn-Blooming Bulbs

Colchicum species and cultivars, especially
'Waterlily'
Crocus goulimyi
Crocus niveus
Cyclamen hederifolium (hardy cyclamen)
Dahlia cultivars
Leucojum autumnale
Nerine bowdenii

Flowers grow best in weed-free, dark rich soil. Shown here: daffodils and a low-growing perennial.

just once a year, that early bloom will quickly fade—and that's all you will get until next year.

You're much better off choosing a smaller plant with lots of buds not quite ready to bloom. Inspect the plant for any evidence of insect or disease problems. You want to see even, healthy growth without disfigured leaves or stems. Slide the plant out of its container. If the roots are curling around and around the bottom of the container, choose another plant; that one has been potbound for too long. Look for good green color and stocky, sturdy growth rather than a plant that is lanky and floppy. The tallest plant is probably not the best choice.

Some perennials ordered through catalogs arrive in bare-root form, meaning that the roots have been harvested after the plant died back in autumn, and the dormant roots are shipped without soil. These roots should be plump with no sign of mildew or rot.

Buying Bulbs
Make sure that the bulbs you buy are healthy. Look for ones that are firm and blemish-free. The larger bulbs of any genus will produce more and larger flowers.

Flower Care

The most important aspect of caring for flowers is to put them in good-quality soil. If you have healthy soil, you will almost be guaranteed healthy plants. (See Chapter 2, pages 13–17, for detailed information on how to create good, productive soil.) Spend the time and money on that job before you invest in plants.

The second basic rule of successful gardening is to choose plants that are well adapted to the environment where you expect them to grow. If you put sun-loving plants in a too-shady setting, you are doomed to frustration. In most cases they will languish, possibly growing leggy and ungainly in search of the

sun and probably not flowering at all. Plants that need a lot of moisture will wither and die in a dry garden, as will plants that hate to have wet feet if they are put in a boggy area.

Buying Perennials and Annuals
When you purchase perennials and annuals in containers, the temptation is to select the plants that are in full bloom. That is a mistake. Those plants have been forced along at a rapid rate and have quickly outgrown their available container space. You risk having long-term problems with roots damaged by being potbound, as well as plants that are exhausted before they've really begun to grow. In the case of perennials that bloom

Shade-tolerant plants growing under dappled light include perennial geranium and hostas.

Choosing Perennials and Annuals

Be a savvy shopper when you are buying perennials and annuals. Be alert to clues about how healthy the plants are. You can tell a lot by a quick inspection of the plant. Here are points to check.

Signs of a Healthy Plant

Good Foliage Color

Symmetrical, Uniform Shape

Well-Branched and Bushy

Plant Size in Proportion to Pot

Securely Attached ID Tag

Only a Few Small Roots Emerging or Visible through Pot Holes

Pot Filled with Soil to within 1" of Rim

Signs of an Unhealthy Plant

Skinny, Irregular Shape

Missing ID Tag

Bent or Broken Shoots

Missing or Discolored Foliage

One or More Thick Roots Coiling Near the Soil Surface

Pot only Partially Filled with Soil

Pot too Small for Plant

One or More Thick Roots Projecting from or Visible through Pot Holes

Choosing Bulbs

Healthy bulbs should be plump and firm. Soft or mushy bulbs are probably rotted. Bulbs that are too light have probably dried out and died. The top mail-order houses will go to great lengths to provide a good-quality product. If you receive a shipment containing bulbs that may not be healthy, call the supplier and let them know. In most cases they will send you replacements free of charge with no questions asked.

Two for the price of one. This double-nosed narcissus bulb will eventually split into two bulbs.

Healthy bulbs should be firm and show some root growth. Avoid those with top growth.

Planting Bulbs

Plant spring-blooming bulbs in the fall around mid or late October once the ground has cooled, in soil that drains well. If you plant too early while the soil is still warm, the bulbs may send up foliage before winter. Depending on the size of the bulbs, they should be buried in 4 to 8 inches of soil. Daffodil bulbs are poisonous to burrowing rodents such as mice, voles, and moles. (The Latin *Narcissus* comes from the root word narcotic.) However, other bulbs, such as tulips and crocus, are very tasty to them. To protect the bulbs, line large planting holes with fine chicken wire, or if you are planting each bulb in a separate hole, toss a handful of sharp gravel in each hole to discourage hungry rodents.

To keep perennial bulbs coming back each year with vigor, fertilize them in the fall when the bulbs are developing their root systems. However, do not put the fertilizer directly into the hole when you plant the bulbs, or you could burn them.

Instead, sprinkle a slow-release plant food over the ground as a topdressing where the bulbs are buried. A spring feeding will also give bulbs an added boost, although the autumn application is more important. Look for a fertilizer that is especially blended for bulbs, with a nutrient ratio such as 5-10-20 and with trace elements listed in the ingredients.

The dying leaves of perennial bulbs should be left undisturbed for at least six weeks to allow the nutrients to flow back into the bulbs. If you tie up or cut back the foliage before six weeks, you'll choke off the needed sunlight and fresh air they need to store sugars for next year's blooms. If you interrupt that process by disturbing the leaves, you'll weaken the bulbs and diminish the blooms you'll get in subsequent years.

Dividing Perennials

Overgrown clumps of perennials won't bloom as prolifically as those with more root room; very old clumps will die in the center, leaving a ring of ailing plant material around the rim. If a perennial bed is densely overgrown, or if the plants in it haven't been divided for some time, it's worth your while to renovate the whole bed and recondition the soil. Remove all the plants to a tarp placed in the shade of a tree. (If there is no nearby shade, cover plants with another tarp to shade them and keep them from drying out.) Spread several inches of compost or well-aged manure and other nutrient-rich organic material over the bed, and dig it in thoroughly. As soon as the bed is ready, divide and replant the perennials, breaking up large clumps of plants and spacing them so that they have room to grow and spread again. As you break up the plant clumps, discard old and woody inner parts. Each new division should have at least two roots and stems. Work as quickly as you can. The longer you leave the plants out of the ground exposed to the drying air, the weaker and more vulnerable they become. (Although some plants, such as irises and daylilies, are farily durable.) If you do need to delay replanting, wrap the plant roots in wet newspapers, and put them out of the sun. Keep the roots moist until you replant.

There are two approaches you can take to the job. The first is to unearth the entire plant and then pull or cut it apart into smaller portions and replant the new bits. The second is to insert your spade firmly into the middle of the clump, cutting it in half while it is in the ground. Then dig out one half, leaving the rest in place. Put fresh soil or a mix of half soil, half compost into the hole left by the plant half that's being removed.

If the plants have been left undivided for too many years, the job isn't always as easy as described above. If the root clump is large, it may take two people tugging with all their might to get it out of the ground. These large root clumps can get so tough and woody that you have to chop them apart with a hatchet.

Shade-tolerant plants growing under dappled light include perennial geranium and hostas.

Dividing Bulbs

Most bulbs, including tubers, rhizomes, and corms, can be divided. In fact, after several years of multiplying underground and becoming more crowded in the process, they benefit from being spaced further apart. Dig up the bulb, pull apart the sections that have developed, and replant. The best time of year for dividing bulbs varies with the type of plant.

Mulching

Flower beds that are cleanly edged and covered with an attractive mulch, such as shredded hardwood bark or cocoa bean hulls, have a pleasingly tidy and finished look. A thick layer of mulch will slow evaporation of moisture from the soil and reduce weeds.

Deadheading and Pinching

Deadheading and pinching may sound like terribly brutal things to do to your flowers, but they are in fact important jobs that help keep the flower garden healthy, beautiful, and productive. Deadheading is simply removing the dead flower heads. Except for the flower heads of a few plants such as *Sedum spectabile*, which look decorative as dried flowers, most are unsightly when they

die. Also, rotting plant debris attracts insects and other pests. Remove spent flowers to keep the garden looking tidy and to maintain the vigor of the plants. In some cases, a perennial will rebloom later in the season if the spent flowers are removed in a timely way.

The generous annuals that flower throughout the season will slow down and eventually stop blooming if the fading flowers aren't removed. Annuals are "programmed" to bloom, set seed, and die. By removing spent flowers before they go to seed, you stimulate the plant to flower again in another effort to produce seed to perpetuate its kind. By deadheading you also stimulate new growth and provide room for the new flowers to grow.

Pinching well-shaped plants is another technique for stimulating new growth. When the plants are 2 to 4 inches high, pinch off the top part of the plant just above the top set of leaves. If the plant has multiple stems or branches, pinch off all the tips. For every branch tip you pinch off, two or three more will grow, and each new branch has the potential to bear flowers. The result of your effort will be a fuller, more floriferous plant. Do not pinch back plants that grow in a low rosette; you'll remove the growing tip.

Deadheading (top left) prevents the plant from producing seeds and encourages more flowering. Shown here: deadheading an *ageratum*.

A mulch of shredded cedar bark (top right) retains moisture and keeps weeds out. Cedar bark is naturally resistant to insects.

Pinching back plants (below) promotes bushy growth and full plants. Whether you use your fingers as shown here or pruners, the process is still called pinching.

Weeds are controlled with a combination of gravel mulch, dense ground covers, and closely spaced plants.

Weeding

Weeds are unsightly, but that is not their worst offense. To survive they have to be aggressive growers, so weeds have adapted to rob nearby plants of all available nutrients and water. If they grow large enough, they'll also hog growing space and light. If they are rampant enough, they may harbor harmful pests and diseases. A weedy garden is an eyesore and an unhealthy environment for any of the plants that you want to grow there.

It is impossible to completely eradicate weeds from the garden. Seeds will blow from the neighbor's garden or even from several blocks away. What the wind doesn't bring, birds may drop into your garden. However, careful maintenance goes a long way toward minimizing the weed problem.

The least labor-intensive approach to weed control is to mulch the garden. If the mulch is laid 4 to 6 inches deep, all but the most aggressive weeds will be stopped. The remainder will be relatively easy to pull. The other secret is to pull weeds before they go to seed. For the trouble of pulling one plant that is going into flower, you halt the potential of literally thousands of new weed plants that could sprout from the resulting seeds. In short, vigilance is your best approach to weed control.

If the weed plants are tiny and you know they aren't seedlings of wanted plants, slice off their roots just below soil level with a sharp hoe. Once they get larger, you're better off digging them out from the roots. Unless they've gone to seed, in which case you should dispose of them in a sealed container, use the pulled weeds as additional mulch, or throw them on the compost heap.

Fertilizing

Even in healthy soil, perennials, annuals, and bulbs need to be fed periodically. After all, plants are continually drawing nutrients out, and at some point those nutrients need to be replenished.

There are two main kinds of fertilizers available: organic and synthetic. Ideally, you want to use organic fertilizer because the synthetic fertilizers, which are produced by industrial processes, contain high concentrations of mineral salts that can acidify the soil and repel earthworms. Do keep in mind, however, that organic fertilizers take longer than synthetics to break down in the soil and become available to plants. Apply them early in the season so that the nutrients are available to the plants when they need it. Because organic fertilizers are less concentrated and release their nutrients slowly, you won't need to apply them as often and you won't need to worry about burning plant roots. Organic fertilizers are less likely to pollute groundwater.

Your best feeding program is to topdress the beds with a couple of inches of compost or aged manure. (See Chapter 2, pages 16-17, for more information on compost and soil amendments.) For people who prefer the convenience of bagged fertilizers, balanced all-purpose organic blends are available. They supply more organic matter than synthetic fertilizers, though less than compost or aged manure. Annuals that bloom all season long, plus a few perennials, may appreciate the extra dose of nutrients that these blends supply. The formulas will be different from those for standard fertilizers because organic blends are generally less concentrated; expect to find formulas such as 4-5-4 or 3-2-2.

Winterizing

Perennials need to be put to bed for winter. After the first frost, cut the plants down to the ground and remove any debris and weeds that could harbor pests and diseases. Also remove annuals at the end of the season. After the first frost kills back their foliage, dig up tender bulbs and store them in a cool, dry place for the winter. Leave ornamental grasses and plants with seed heads, which make an attractive winter display. Those plants should be cut down in early spring to allow room for new growth to develop.

Mulch with Evergreen Boughs to Prevent Heaving. In climates where winter heaving can uproot perennials, exposing roots to cold and drought, wait until the ground freezes for the first time. Then apply a layer of loose (nonmatting) mulch or evergreen boughs to help keep the ground frozen so it remains stable.

Although most plants will continue to grow throughout winter in warm climates, autumn is a good time to give the beds a good tidying. Remove the tired leaves from plants such as irises, and rake out any fallen leaves or debris. While you're at it, take the time to remove weeds. Once winter or spring rains start, they'll begin growing vigorously. Pull weeds out when they're young, and certainly before they go to seed.

Look for the Beauty in Winter.

Although many gardeners spend the winter dreaming of spring, there is something to be said for appreciating the quiet stillness of the winter landscape. If your landscape has good bones, it should have enough structure that it won't look bare during the winter.

Take a mental picture of your garden before you cut everything back. Remember how it looked in its spring glory. Use this slow season to catch up on your records, making note of which plants worked and which you'd like to move in the spring. If there is nothing interesting to look at from inside, plan to plant a tree or shrub (preferably one with winter interest) to fill in the gap in your garden view.

Shop the Catalogs with Purpose.

After you've created your wish list, start browsing through garden catalogs. Refer back to your notes, and think about the conditions in your garden. Then you can shop the catalogs with purpose, and you won't be tempted with impulse purchases.

Keep your gardening gloves handy. And when that warm day comes in February, as it always does, get outside and poke around, looking and listening for signs of spring.

Put perennials to bed for the winter. After the first frost, lay evergreen boughs over plants to prevent heaving. The boughs keep the ground frozen.

After a killing frost, cut perennial plants down to the ground. After such a frost, the stems of herbaceous plants will turn black and mushy. Take time to appreciate the tranquility of this moment before cutting things back.

zone maps

Average Annual Minimum Temperature

Temp. (°C)	Zone	Temp. (°F)
−45.6 & below	1	below −50
−42.8 to −45.5	2a	−45 to −50
−40.0 to −42.7	2b	−40 to −45
−37.3 to −40.0	3a	−35 to −40
−34.5 to −37.2	3b	−30 to −35
−31.7 to −34.4	4a	−25 to −30
−28.9 to −31.6	4b	−20 to −25
−26.2 to −28.8	5a	−15 to −20
−23.4 to −26.1	5b	−10 to −15
−20.6 to −23.3	6a	−5 to −10
−17.8 to −20.5	6b	0 to −5
−15.0 to −17.7	7a	5 to 0
−12.3 to −15.0	7b	10 to 5
−9.5 to −12.2	8a	15 to 10
−6.7 to −9.4	8b	20 to 15
−3.9 to −6.6	9a	25 to 20
−1.2 to −3.6	9b	30 to 25
1.6 to −1.1	10a	35 to 30
4.4 to 1.7	10b	40 to 35
4.5 & above	11	40 & above

The USDA Hardiness Map divides North America into 11 zones according to average minimum winter temperatures. Hardiness zones are used to identify regions to which plants are suited based on their cold tolerance, which is what "hardiness" means. Many factors, such as elevation and moisture level, come into play when determining whether a plant is suitable for your region. Local climates may vary from what is shown on this map. Contact your local Cooperative Extension Service for recommendations for your area.

Plant Hardiness Zones

0a	4a
0b	4b
1a	5a
1b	5b
2a	6a
2b	6b
3a	7a
3b	7b
	8a

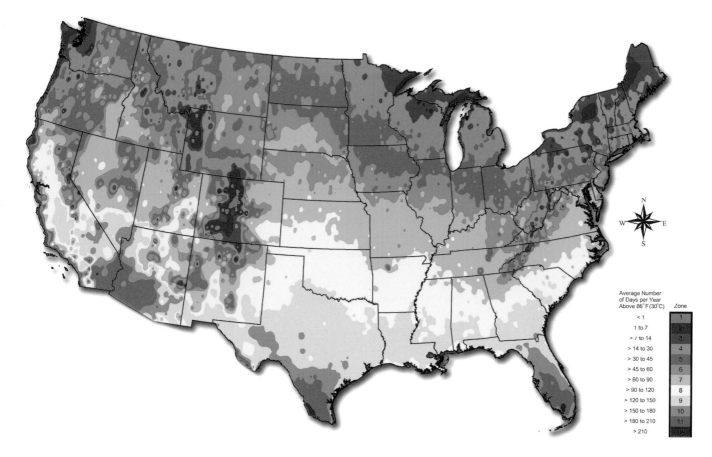

Average Number of Days per Year Above 86°F (30°C)	Zone
< 1	1
1 to 7	2
> 7 to 14	3
> 14 to 30	4
> 30 to 45	5
> 45 to 60	6
> 60 to 90	7
> 90 to 120	8
> 120 to 150	9
> 150 to 180	10
> 180 to 210	11
> 210	12

The American Horticultural Society Heat-Zone Map divides the United States into 12 zones based on the average annual number of days a region's temperatures climb above 86°F (30°C), the temperature at which the cellular proteins of plants begin to experience injury. Introduced in 1998, the AHS Heat-Zone Map holds significance, especially for gardeners in southern and transitional zones. Nurseries, growers, and other plant sources will gradually begin listing both cold hardiness and heat tolerance zones for plants, including grass plants. Using the USDA Plant Hardiness map, which can help determine a plant's cold tolerance, and the AHS Heat-Zone Map, gardeners will be able to safely choose plants that tolerate their region's lowest and highest temperatures.

Canada's Plant Hardiness Zone Map outlines the different zones in Canada where various types of trees, shrubs, and flowers will most likely survive. It is based on the average climatic conditions of each area. The hardiness map is divided into nine major zones: the harshest is 0 and the mildest is 8. Relatively few plants are suited to zone 0. Subzones (e.g., 4a or 4b, 5a or 5b) are also noted in the map legend. These subzones are most familiar to Canadian gardeners. Some significant local factors, such as micro-topography, amount of shelter, and subtle local variations in snow cover, are too small to be captured on the map. Year-to-year variations in weather and gardening techniques can also have a significant impact on plant survival in any particular location.

glossary

Apical dominance The tendency of the top stems or branches to inhibit the development of lateral, or side, shoots because of the concentration of growth hormone in branch tips.

Apex (Plural: apices) The tip (tips) of branches or the end buds of a growing plant.

Aslar Stone cut at a quarry to produce smooth, flat bedding surfaces that stack easily. Walls made from such stones have a formal appearance.

Base map A drawing or survey that details the location of all property boundaries, structures, slopes, significant plantings, and location of sunrise and sunset. An important first step in landscaping.

Bed joint Hortizontal masonry joint, as opposed to a vertical masonry joint (called a head joint). Also called beds.

Berm A mound of earth that directs or retains water. A 6-inch berm built around the drip line of a tree or shrub will create a basin, ensuring that water reaches the plant's roots.

Bond stones Support stones that extend through the full thickness of a wall. They are staggered and placed every few feet along the length of the wall for extra strength.

Cap The top, flat layer of a masonry structure. Often ornamental, it also keeps out water, thus preventing the expansion and contraction caused by freezing and thawing of water caught in the seams. Also known as coping.

Collar The slight swelling that occurs where a branch of a tree or shrub meets the trunk. Also known as the saddle.

Footing The concrete base that supports a masonry wall or other structure. It is built below the local frost line to prevent heaving.

Genus (plural: genera) A closely related group of species sharing similar characteristics and probably evolved from the same ancestors. In scientific, or botanical, language the genus name begins with a capital letter and is followed by the species name, which begins with a lowercase letter. Both words are italicized, as in *Acer palmatum*.

Hardscape Parts of a landscape constructed from materials other than plants, such as walks, walls, and trellises, made of wood, stone, or other materials.

Jointing The finish given to the mortar that extrudes from each course of bricks.

Parterre Diminutive hedges, such as boxwood, used to divide space and serve as decorative frames for other plantings in formal gardens.

Plat Prepared by professional surveyors, it shows precise property lines and any easements. It is used for making a base map for landscaping and is available from a tax assessor's office or given to homeowners when purchasing their property.

Reinforcing rod Steel bar inside the concrete foundation of a wall used for extra support.

Softscape The palette of plants used in a landscape, as opposed to the hardscape, which refers to non-living landscape objects such as paths, stones, patios, and walls.

Species Among plants, a group that shares many characteristics, including essential flower types, and that can interbreed freely. In scientific, or botanical, language the species name always follows the genus name and begins with a lowercase letter. Both words are italicized, as in *Acer palmatum*.

Swale A naturally occurring wetland area where water tends to flow or accumulate during heavy rains.

Weep holes Holes that allow water to seep through a retaining wall so that it does not build up behind the wall.

Wythe A vertical section of a wall that is equal to the width of the masonry unit.

Xeriscape Landscape design that utilizes drought-tolerant plants and various techniques for minimizing water use.

index

index

photo credits